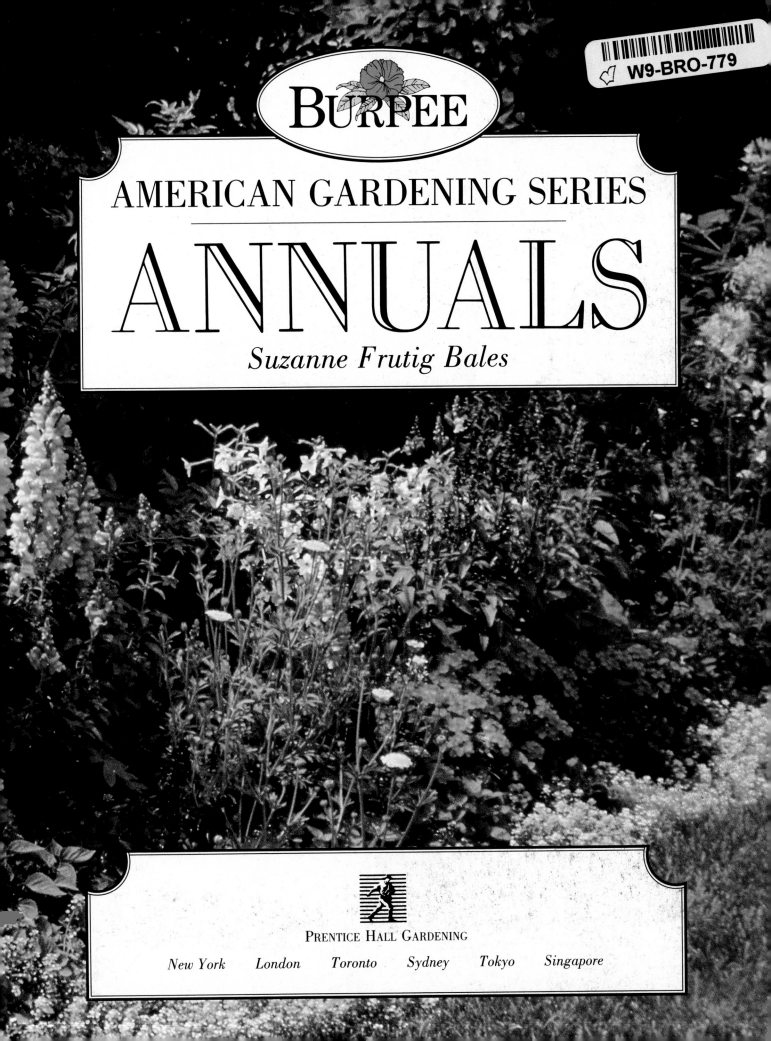

BURPEE

AMERICAN GARDENING SERIES

ANNUALS

Suzanne Frutig Bales

PRENTICE HALL GARDENING

New York   London   Toronto   Sydney   Tokyo   Singapore

This book is dedicated to my father, Edward C. Frutig, whose help and encouragement made it possible.

PRENTICE HALL GENERAL REFERENCE
15 Columbus Circle
New York, NY 10023

PRENTICE HALL and colophon are registered trademarks of Simon & Schuster, Inc.

BURPEE is a registered trademark of W. Atlee Burpee & Company.

Library of Congress Cataloging in Publication Data

Bales, Suzanne Frutig.
   The Burpee American gardening series. Annuals / Suzanne Frutig Bales.
      p.   cm.
   ISBN 0-671-86394-0
   1. Annuals (Plants)   2. Annuals (Plants)—Pictorial works.
 I. Title.   II. Title: Annuals.
 SB422.B285   1991
 635.9′312—dc20   90-34512
                                                    CIP

Designed by Patricia Fabricant
Manufactured in the United States of America

9 8 7 6 5 4

First Edition January 1991

PHOTOGRAPHY CREDITS

Agricultural Research Service, USDA
American Takii, Inc.
Bales, Suzanne Frutig
Ball Seed Co.
Denholm Seeds
Dibblee, Steven
Floranova Ltd.
Gitts, Nicholas, of Swan Island Dahlias
Horticultural Photography, Corvallis, Oregon
Kieft Bloemzaden B.V.
Old Sturbridge Village, Sturbridge, Massachusetts
PanAmerican Seed Co.
Reynolds, Kurt, Goldsmith Seeds, Inc.
Rokach, Allen
Royal Sluis
Sakata Seed America, Inc.

Drawings by Michael Gale

I am happy to finally express my deep gratitude to the many people who have helped me while I was writing this book. My thanks go to Gina Norgard, Martha Kraska and my husband and partner, Carter F. Bales, for providing me with unending help, support and love and to Alice R. Ireys, my close friend and mentor.

I greatly appreciate the help of two wonderful friends and consultants: Allan Armitage and Wayne Winterrowd.

I am indebted to horticulturists Chela Kleiber, Eileen Kearney, Steve Frowine, Carol Whitenack, Charles Cresson, Jim Hoge and Ralph Borchard; to the Burpee breeders Dr. Dennis Flaschenreim, Teresa Jacobsen, John J. Mondry, Dr. Nung Che Chen, Dr. Michael Burke and Lois Stringer; to Jonathan Burpee and the Burpee customer service department; and to photography coordinator Barbara Wolverton and administrative assistant Elda Malgieri.

At Prentice Hall I would like to thank Anne Zeman, publisher, editor and gardener, whose watchful eye, patience, enthusiasm and belief in these books have made them a reality; Rebecca Atwater, whose twist of a phrase and change of a word have greatly improved and polished these books; Rachel Simon for her patience and thoroughness.

Cover: At Old Sturbridge Village, the practical herb purple ruffled basil is beautifully combined with tall cleomes and malvas; the border is edged with vincas.

Preceding pages: This gently curved annual border has the look of an established planting. Airy cleomes stand behind snapdragons, nicotianas, phlox and salvias. Alyssums provide a soft edging.

CONTENTS

THE ANNUAL GARDEN PLANNER

THE ALL-PURPOSE FLOWER

It was with annuals that my love of gardening began and I invite them back into the garden each year like old friends. Their long bloom, wide color range, and easy care make them welcome guests. Annuals are God's gift to gardeners. They are the most popular plants grown in American gardens. They are also the most forgiving of plants, for they tolerate a wide range of conditions while splashing color throughout the garden. Annuals are the flowers that bloom the first season from seeds sown in the spring and give many months of continuous bloom before going to seed or being killed by heavy frost and winter weather.

Annuals are practical too. A new home can be landscaped at a modest cost with young, inexpensive shrubs supplemented with annuals; the flowers give a full, more finished look while the shrubs grow and fill out. Spilling from window boxes, annuals add warmth and charm to the exterior of a house. They dress up and enliven a terrace or patio. An unpleasing view, a crumbling wall, an unpainted fence, the neighbor's shed, all can be hidden with annual vines or transformed by groupings of annuals into an area of beautiful, pleasing color.

Annuals have been called the "bright gems of nature" because of their wide, bright range of colors: the neon orange of poppies, the brazen scarlet of celosias, the blood red of coleuses, the flamingo pink of geraniums. A friend refers to these as the "sixty-mile-an-hour flowers." Driving at that speed you can spot them. How-

ever, annuals come in all colors and shades, including pastels and soft, translucent colors. The colors of annuals differ from those of bulbs, perennials, and flowering trees. None is so bold as annuals are.

As a bonus, no matter where or why you plant annuals, they furnish abundant blooms for bringing indoors in bouquets or for giving to friends and neighbors.

For convenience, annuals are grouped into three categories: **hardy, half-hardy,** and **tender.** The way a seed or young plant is handled will vary according to the category to which it belongs. **Hardy annuals** are the annuals whose seedlings are able to survive freezing weather. They can be sown in the fall or in the early spring as soon as the ground can be worked. Most hardy annuals do not tolerate heat and bloom early in the spring, continuing until killed by hot summer weather. Larkspur (*Consolida orientalis*), forget-me-not (*Myosotis* species), and pansies (*Viola* × *wittrockiana*) are all good examples of hardy annuals.

Half-hardy annuals are sown after all danger of frost in the spring and, once established, can survive light frost in the fall but will die from a heavy frost or prolonged cold spell. In my Zone 7 garden, (see The USDA Plant Hardiness Map on page 94), I am still picking salvias, scabiosas, and cosmos for bouquets in early December.

Tender annuals are the most fragile of flowers and can be planted only in a warm soil.

Mixing herbs with annuals makes a beautiful and practical design. The purple ruffled basil enhances the pink of cleomes, malvas, and periwinkle, and can also be used in cooking.

Annuals for Partial Shade

Abutilon	Lobularia (sweet alyssum)
Ageratum	
	Mimulus
Begonia	
	Mirabilis (four-o'clock)
Browallia	
	Molucella (bells-of-Ireland)
Catharanthus (periwinkle)	
	Myosotis (forget-me-not)
Celosia	
Clarkia (farewell-to-spring)	Nicotiana
	Nierembergia
Coleus	
	Pelargonium (geranium)
Dahlia	
Helianthus (sunflower)	Perilla
	Salpiglossis
Heliotropium	
Hypoestes	Torenia (wishbone flower)
Impatiens	
	Tropaeolum (nasturium)
Lathyrus	
Lisianthus	Viola (pansy)
Lobelia	

Above: Begonias add a splash of color to a shady spot under a tree.

They will not survive even a light frost. So, let the ground warm before planting amaranths, begonias, celosias, impatiens, and other tender annuals.

Annual seeds, regardless of their plant classification, can survive freezing but most will rot in cold, damp, rainy conditions. Annuals frequently reseed themselves, although not necessarily where you want them. But finding plants in unexpected places adds to the gardener's joy and sense of discovery. In my garden, petunias are growing between the cracks of our stone walk, having sprinted six feet from where they grew last year. Cleome seeds have leaped a 5-foot wall and are blooming among my perennials. One lone sunflower stands tall under a tree where my bird feeder hung last winter; quite a feat, escaping the hungry birds, growing in clay, and blooming in shade. White alyssum that started as an edging for my shrub roses is now more of a groundcover; the roses appear to bloom on a white cloud, and I love it.

All are happy accidents of nature.

Rain, snow, wind, and birds may move seeds about, surprising gardeners by where they take root and grow, but it is best to replant deliberately with fresh seeds each spring. This is especially the case in northern climates, because annual seeds, planted in the fall, are frequently moved by the elements and cannot be depended on to grow where they have been sown.

It is nice to know that there is an annual to fill perfectly the need for a spot of color anywhere in your garden or around your home. There is an annual appropriate for every place and every growing condition. You need only match the plant to the place; it is easier than you might think, and this book will help you. Gardeners get into trouble when they mismatch a plant and its setting, not because they have a black thumb. There is no such thing as a green or black thumb. Anyone can be successful by learning the needs of individual plants and planting accordingly.

ANNUALS AS AN EDGING

A sweeping curve of flowers along a walk greets and cheers visitors. The straight line to a back door can be dressed and softened with flowers spilling onto the path. A foundation planting, scalloped with annuals, is pleasing to the eye, setting off the lines of the house and bringing a finished look to your landscape.

Using annuals to edge a perennial border adds shape and continuity too; they tie together the perennials that bloom in succession. You can use one annual continuously or, if you feel more adventuresome, plant two in a pattern so that they weave in and out of one another, front and back, forming colorful blending loops. In the picture of the nautical garden on page 9, alyssums and ageratums were alternated. Both bloom all summer and the blue and white colors pleasingly complement each other.

ANNUALS ARE GREAT FOR SHADE

Just looking at a shady spot on a hot, sunny day can be refreshing. Now imagine it full of colorful impatiens in full bloom. It becomes even more refreshing.

An area in partial shade will have three or four hours of full sun each day. Begonias prefer partial shade, as do impatiens. Impatiens, the most popular bedding plant in America, love a certain amount of shade and are easy to grow. They come in a wide assortment of colors and combinations of colors, need no deadheading (pinching off of the dead flowers), and bloom straight from late spring through summer and fall until heavy frost. Try Burpee's most popular impatiens mix—the 'Rosette Hybrid Mix'. The exquisite double flowers look like miniature roses.

The lesser known torenias provide cheery color for a partially shady spot. The tubular flowers of 'Clown Mix' are splashed with violets, pinks, and blues. A single spot of yellow at the mouth of the flower resembles a tongue. Their name holds true, and I am always reminded of clowns and smile when I pass them.

Other annuals that thrive in partial shade include tall, spidery cleomes, fragrant nicotianas, delicate, jewel-like lobelias, star-shaped browallias, fluffy, feathery celosias, spiky larkspurs, and the early blooming, old-fashioned pansies.

There are many more, and you'll have the pleasure of combining them and trying new ones each year. Some flowers do better in one part of the country than another. It is fun to experiment to see which are best for your soil, climate, and above all, your personal taste.

If for some reason a flower you like doesn't perform well the first time you plant it, don't give up. There are many variables that affect a plant's performance; turn to page 83 for some help identifying just what the problem might be. An unusually heavy rainy season may dampen the results of a specific plant. The following year, rainfall may be normal and your plant will bloom and bloom and bloom. Experiment—and enjoy.

This nautical garden by the sea is defined by winding dusty miller that resembles a twisting of heavy ship's rope.

ANNUALS WITH BULBS

Opposite, from top: Mother Nature doesn't separate annuals from perennials—why should we? Annuals cheerfully fill the spaces between perennials for a "fuller" garden.

Second photograph: Cool-weather-loving pansies are wonderful around and under spring-blooming tulips; the pansies will continue to bloom long after the tulips have died back.

Third photograph: This colorful and arresting border is filled with lime green coleuses and with the dark foliage and bright pink flowers of New Guinea impatiens.

Bottom: Vines, such as this morning glory, are a dramatic backdrop for gardens, making them appear larger.

Beginning gardeners make a common mistake: they plant bulbs exactly as the planting guides instruct, and then are disappointed the first years because the garden looks so spare. Planting guides are written to allow bulbs, perennials, and shrubs room to expand over a period of years, and that does not make for the best effect right after planting. Daffodils, tulips, and most flowering bulbs look lonely when planted 8 to 10 inches apart, as guides usually recommend. It is the brown open soil that catches the eye as much as the flower. There are solutions, however. Plant closer, and plant cold-weather annuals like forget-me-nots (*Myosotis*), which blooms at the same time as tulips and continues blooming after the tulips are gone. Plant

these seeds in the fall at the same time as the bulbs go in, and position them right over your bulbs. The next spring you'll be delighted to see your tulips dancing in a sea of tiny blue flowers. The roots of forget-me-nots are shallow and won't interfere with the tulips, the roots of which are eight inches or more below the surface.

Forget-me-nots is only one of many cold-weather annuals that can be planted with bulbs; refer to the chart on page 91 for suggestions. You have a wealth of choices: pansies are a wonderful annual. They bloom in time to complement tulips and continue blooming until the hot nights of summer lull them to sleep. In southern states, pansies bloom all winter. In northern states they can be planted

in the fall in a cold frame for protection from heavy snow. They winter over nicely and can be moved to the garden in the spring. Light frost will not dampen their spirit.

In the late spring, the foliage of tulips and daffodils yellows and dies back. The foliage should not be removed because it is storing energy for setting next year's bloom. Nevertheless these unattractive beds can be camouflaged by impatiens, marigolds, geraniums, vincas, or another of your favorite annuals. The shallow roots of the annuals cannot disturb the bulbs in their deep nest. By the same token, the bulbs are dormant during the summer and will not compete with the annuals for nutrients. The result is continuous and colorful bloom.

ANNUALS WITH PERENNIALS

Perennial flowers, once planted, bloom in the garden year after year. Each succeeding year they produce more flowers and cover a larger area. They start small, rarely blooming the first year, and it takes time for them to completely cover the area you have chosen for them. Planted

in the bare areas between perennials, annuals quickly hide the soil with their fast-growing, full-flowered beauty. As the perennials grow over the following years, fewer annuals will be needed to fill in. Eventually, the perennials will grow enough to decorate the area

unassisted.

Annuals can also be effectively mixed with a border of perennials, again, to give continuous bloom to the border, wherever one perennial stops flowering and before another starts.

ANNUALS GROWN FOR FOLIAGE

Annuals grown for foliage can light up a shady spot or enhance a sunny garden as well as their flowering cousins. The leaves of coleuses come in wild and bold color combinations: burgundy with lime green, dark green with pink and yellow,

and exuberant shades of red. Snow-on-the-mountain (*Euphorbia marginata*) appears to be covered with snow and makes for a very cooling summer scene. The polka-dot plant (*Hypoestes phyllostachya*) is eye-catching with its splashed pink or white spots.

Flower shoots should be removed from the plants as soon as they are formed by these foliage plants. The flowers are insignificant, and removing them keeps the plants from going to seed and dying back.

ANNUAL VINES

Vines are underutilized, often overlooked by gardeners. They shouldn't be; they are easy to grow, require only a square foot of ground space, and can rise 8 feet and more in a single season, adding drama and beauty to a garden of any size.

These talented plants are valuable even in a small garden, where they create an illusion of size. Vines mask unsightly buildings and can hide all sorts of imperfections when grown on a fence, wall, trellis, or arbor. Vines can be your background or stage set for the garden in the foreground. Their effect can be to tie the entire garden together, drawing attention to the beauty of your flowers.

Several vines can be woven together on the same arbor, fence, or trellis to give a tapestry effect. You can plant vines that bloom together or at different times to complement each other. Even various shades of green foliage woven together creates interesting patterns. Two that work well together are hyacinth bean (*Dolichos lablab*) grown for its burgundy beans and flowers, and moonflower (*Ipomoea alba*), grown for its fragrance and large white trumpet flowers that open and glow at dusk. Morning glories, always a favorite, can be grown in single colors or in multicolors to add sparkle.

Vines need not always grow vertically. They can be very effective scrambling over the ground, hanging off a bank, climbing over a nonflowering shrub or tree, or even winding around a tall sunflower. Annual vines grown in the North are short-lived and do not damage their support plant. Annual vines that like growing conditions in the South can reach considerable height and cover larger areas, sometimes needing to be pruned to fit their space well.

Vines climb by different methods. Some twist around supports, while others have tendrils that grab hold of supports. Check to make sure you know the method used by the vine you want to grow, so you give it the help it needs to do what you want it to do. Simply being planted next to a fence is enough for such vines as morning glories, hyacinth beans, and scarlet runner beans.

Some annual vines that pull themselves up by tendrils, such as morning glories or moonflowers, can even be grown over sturdy perennial vines like climbing roses to bloom in mid- and late summer when rose blossoms are scarce. The climbing rose can act as a trellis for the annual vine to cling to and climb on. The rose thorns won't bother the vine at all.

DESIGNING AN ANNUAL GARDEN

When we first moved, our property had a tumble-down wall covered by ivy. It would have been best to rebuild the wall immediately, but time and money were at a premium, and eleven years passed before we got around to taking it down. I wanted a perennial garden in front of it but, being practical, I wasn't going to spend the amount of money it would require and add the extra work of moving the plants when we replaced the wall at a later date. Annuals were the answer. I planned and planted the garden as though I had been using perennials, with a curving front, deep width (5 feet), varied heights rising to 5 feet at the back, and using my favorite colors pink, blue, and white. It was easier than planning a perennial garden because all of the flowers bloomed together for three months or longer. (Most perennials bloom for several weeks and the garden has to be planned for successive blooms, as the plants never bloom all at once.) Many of our visitors mistakenly believed I had a perennial garden simply because they had seen annuals planted only as carpets, with no variation in height.

Every year I replanted this garden in almost the same design, with the same flowers in the same spots, breaking the first rule of gardening: rotate the plants. But I was careful in preparing the garden, adding an abundance of compost and peat moss each year, and had few problems. I photographed the garden each year but never looked back from year to year and compared the changes until recently. The changes were subtle. More pink has crept in, some deeper rose even bordering on red, and the white is washing out. What really is noticeable is that the garden did indeed look considerably better over time. As a gardener I learned and improved, without being very aware of it. What is surprising is that I remember this garden as being my favorite, the easiest garden right from the beginning. Success in gardening should be measured in the pleasure it gives the gardener. Even when my garden looks scraggly, I am rewarded with a few flowers to bring into the house.

Gardening is like anything else: the more you do it, the more you learn, and the quicker and easier the process becomes. Initially, it takes more time and effort to break up the ground and prepare a new garden but the following years are easier. The first year, every garden needs extra maintenance. As you learn which plants grow well for you and the requirements of those plants, your garden will require less care.

An annual garden planted in the style of a classic perennial border, featuring tall cleomes in the back, snapdragons, salvias, and nicotianas in the middle, and verbenas in the front.

Planning: Six Easy Steps

Plan before you plant and you will avoid the mistakes that come from haphazard planting and have a more successful, pleasing garden design. The following list will help you begin:

1. Repetition can work to your advantage: One way to achieve unity is to repeat the same group of flowers several times, evenly or randomly, throughout the border.

2. Plant in threes or more of each plant. If you plant fewer than three of one plant together, the effect will be stingy and spotty.

3. Organize by height. Put the tallest plants at the back, the shortest at the front. However, on occasion, don't be afraid to add a surprise by letting a tall plant fill in an area all the way to the front of the border.

4. Don't be rigid. Masses of single color of one variety overlapping and weaving into the mass of another variety can be most attractive. If you plant in rows or blocks of color, however, the smallest imperfection will draw attention. One flower leaning on its neighbor will look out of place.

5. Plan your colors. If you are unsure how to combine colors, choose a combination of two or three from Color in the Garden (page 16) and stick to it. Look over the colors used in the photographs in this book, and use the color combinations that you like best.

6. Which varieties? There are hundreds of species of annuals and thousands of varieties within those species. In our "Plant Portraits," beginning on page 37, we cover the easiest and most readily available varieties. This is a good starting place. If you are a new gardener, you might begin with the plants marked "easy," as they require the least knowledge and care.

TO BEGIN

Planning a garden takes the same thought and planning as decorating the rooms in your home. Even if you do all your decorating at once, during the year you acquire new things or move the furniture around. The same is true with gardens. Gardeners think about dividing their property into garden "rooms": areas for entertaining, for childrens' play, a quiet place for reading, and welcoming flowers at the front of the house. Each area need not be large but should be designed separately and complement the others.

Think about your family's lifestyle. Will you entertain or eat in your garden? Is it a garden to view from a terrace, porch, or window? Do you want to be able to pick fragrant flowers throughout the summer? Do you want flowers to dry and bring in for long winter color? Would you like edible flowers to garnish summer drinks and salads?

When you have thought about what you want, walk around your property. Where is the best area to plant? Is it a corner garden, a border in front of a hedge or fence, or an island bed cut into the lawn near the house? Each of these shapes has different possibilities.

Before you dig, outline the garden area with lime or stakes connected by string. Look at the shape and size. It is better to have a small, well-maintained garden than a larger, messy one, so don't select an area too large for you to maintain comfortably. You can enlarge it later, if you like. Besides, a garden will look larger once planted and filled with mature plants in full color.

Next, consider whether it is possible to achieve what you have in mind in the area available. The best way to know for sure is to measure. After you have measured your garden, draw it on graph paper, using a scale of ¼ inch to 1 foot. This will tell you how many plants you need and where to put them for the best effect. The smaller plants at the front of the border need to be spaced approximately 6 inches apart; middle-of-the-border plants need to be approximately 8 to 12 inches apart, and the taller plants at the back are best spaced 24 to 36 inches. Check the spacing in "Plant Portraits," page 37. Your border will need to be at least 4 feet wide if you want to back it with large 4- to 6-foot plants.

The plants should be planted in triangles. Straight lines look too rigid. The idea is to have the plants close enough so they grow together, hide the soil, and seem to flow from one to another.

SELECTING YOUR PLANTS

Seed catalogs arrive in early winter and contain hundreds of different varieties of flowers. They are a relaxing and easy way to expand your knowledge of plants and a good place to start planning your garden.

On a snowy Saturday afternoon, warmed by a flaming fire, planning next season's garden is one of my favorite things. Many ideas come from browsing through the new seed catalogs. They are always overflowing with new plants and gardening hints. I never really mind that my garden doesn't look quite as I planned, or that most of my plans are never executed; the pleasure of dreaming is often enough. Ultimately the knowledge that comes from reading influences and improves my garden for the coming season.

Plants have personalities. Some are easy guests, adjusting to a wide range of conditions. Others are demanding, fussy, and difficult. Check in "Plant Portraits," page 37, or your garden catalogs to get acquainted with the personalities of your favorite plants.

To be successful, choose plants not for their beauty alone. You must select the ones that will grow and thrive in the conditions in your garden. By understanding your site, your climate, and soil, you can match the plant to the place. If you put a plant in unfavorable conditions, it will disappoint you and not perform to its full potential.

SUN OR SHADE: How many hours a day does the sun shine on your garden site? Select plants that thrive in those conditions. Forcing plants into conditions that are not favorable will lead to wasted time and money.

SOIL: Some annuals tolerate sandy or poorer soils lacking in minerals and organic matter. And some will grow in clay, but most need a rich soil with good drainage. What kind of soil are you starting with?

HABIT: Habit refers to the shape and form of a plant. Consider whether you want plants that spill out over the ground, form bushy mounds, are spiky skyscrapers, or climb vertically to create tapestry backgrounds. You can mix them all.

BLOOM TIME: All annuals do not grow from seed at the same rate. Some take a matter of weeks to bloom (alyssums, *Gypsophila* 'Covent Garden White', nasturtiums, and marigolds, to name a few). Others can take from 4 to 6 months until they are ready to bloom (geraniums, begonias, and dahlias, for example). When planting the later-blooming varieties from seed, start them indoors early enough so they'll be ready to transplant outdoors at the proper time. If you are buying your plants from a nursery, they will have been started indoors at the proper time to insure that they will bloom shortly after being planted in your garden.

FORM: Does the flower have a sculptural solid form (dahlia, sunflower, zinnia) or is it a delicate filigree dome of florets (love-in-a-mist, blue lace flower, baby's breath)? Alternating different forms in the same color can add interest and beauty to your garden.

FOLIAGE: There are many different colors available, and foliage color ought to be considered just as flower color is. Look for foliage that will blend with the flowers in your border. Foliage can be as subtle as the white-veined leaves of euphorbia or as bright as the reddish-purple foliage of perilla or the deep purple of begonias and New Guinea impatiens.

The greens vary, too. There are many different shades of green, from the lime green of the bells-of-Ireland to the medium green of cosmos or the dark green of periwinkle. Leaves come in a variety of shapes (oval, round, heart, spidery, or willowy), sizes (from tiny to enormous) and textures (waxy, smooth, or even hairy). Mother Nature has somehow arranged it so that plants rarely clash outdoors and if you don't like the combination you have planted, that is easy enough to change. Annuals don't have deep roots and most do not mind transplanting, when it's done with care at the proper time.

COLOR IN THE GARDEN

Of all plant and garden characteristics, that with the most immediate impact is color. Color establishes the mood of the garden. You can create a quiet place, a cool corner, a romantic nook, or even add surprise and drama to your garden, all through the use of color. Color can be used to create illusions and make a garden look bigger, smaller, wider, or deeper. Pastel or lighter colors, because they make individual blossoms harder to distinguish, tend to create a sense of distance and make a garden seem larger. Strong colors, which are easier to see even at great distances, appear to be closer and consequently make a garden seem smaller.

The use of color is a personal thing. Your garden should contain your favorites. Planning color in a garden is similar to planning or coordinating a wardrobe, where you probably would not combine all the colors available. It is easier to create a pleasing garden by blending a few colors. Aim for colors that harmonize and complement each other.

Random color placement can create a shootout among many bold and brightly colored flowers. A restless mood prevails and is hard on the eyes. This is where good planning is important. Use the foliage of the flowers, with different shades of green as a framework to create a flow from one color to the next, weaving the colors together.

Silver foliage plants can act as mediators and make peace between flowers, the colors of which would otherwise fight, thus providing a quiet and cooling transition to the more exuberant colors. They can also draw attention to flowers by highlighting them with a halo of silver, making light-colored flowers appear darker.

A warm garden is created with such warm colors as reds, oranges, and yellows. However, a word of caution is necessary when planning with red. Red is the most difficult color to combine. As one gardener says, it can "burn a hole" in any color scheme. Intense and bright, it draws the eye and overpowers the other colors in the garden. One solution is to plant red with orange and yellow, because they can hold their own against such a strong partner. In general, the more brilliant a color, the less of it you need.

A cool garden is created by using cooler colors: blues, white, and silver. Blue in flower color can mean any color from violet to lilac and purple, as there are few true blue flowers. These colors have an air of coolness about them that benefits the gardener in the hottest months of July and August. A blue and white garden repeats and reflects the sky and the clouds. (It is also one of the most popular color combinations for china and pottery.) Blue and white is always a winning combination.

A romantic garden uses an abundance of pinks and pastels on light, airy foliage. The flowers float and move with the breezes. There is nothing formal, nothing stiff. One plant weaves into another.

The depth and intensity of colors change with the rising and the setting of the sun. On a bright sunny day, color in a garden becomes washed out and faded. If you sit in your garden as twilight approaches, however, you will notice the flower colors brighten, until dusk settles and darkness covers all but the white flowers. White flowers, like white clothing at night, hold the light and glow even in the dusk and early evening. If you entertain in the evenings in your garden, you should consider planting many different white flowers to create a moonlight garden.

A moonlight garden is one of the earliest documented American ornamental gardens. One was grown in Massachusetts in 1833. They are so beautiful that it is surprising there are few today. When combined with the fragrance that many white flowers have, and when seen in the early evening, a sea of white flowers is hard to forget. However, most of us would have trouble sacrificing all of the wonderful flower colors available for a single color. It may be easier to plant all-white flowers in containers on a terrace, or in one area that is a favorite evening spot, leaving other areas for more colorful planting. Use white flowers mixed with light-colored flowers for greater visibility at night to outline a path.

An all-white garden, or any one-color garden for that matter, need not be boring. There are many possibilities and unusual combinations. Two or more flowers of the same color, but with very different shapes, can make an interesting planting.

For example, try mixing the delicate, tiny-flowered white alyssum with the strong sculptural shape of white grandiflora petunias and white trumpets of nicotiana. *Zinnia* 'Rose Pinwheel' combines nicely with the delicate foliage and flower shape of pink love-in-a-mist (*Nigella damascena*) and the spiky, solid structure of pink snapdragons (*Antirrhinum* species). Rounding a corner to see the surprise of a bold planting of *Zinnia* 'Scarlet Splendor' surrounded by red nicotianas can take your breath away.

Two-color gardens can also be very easy to plan. Popular colors that work well together are blue and pink, orange and yellow, blue and yellow, red and white, purple and orange, and blue and white. White and green can be combined with any color. Again, remember to vary the shapes and habits of the flowers for interest and variety. There is no limit to the number of different flowers of the same colors you can plant together. Just remember to plant at least three plants of one variety together. If you're planting dwarf plants, more is better.

It is, of course, possible to design a rainbow garden or a many-colored carpet of blooms, but select the colors and the order in which they appear with care. White, yellow, orange, red, scarlet, purple and blue, follow one another nicely. Orange and pink do not, and should not be planted next to each other.

Above all, don't be intimidated by color in the garden. Think of color as an acquaintance, someone you want to get to know better. You have the opportunity to develop a long and supportive friendship! Start simply, be observant, and experiment over time. All your life you have been using color and reacting to it, from noticing a friend's new clothes, to selecting colors for a car, a house, a new rug. If you are like most people, your favorite color has changed from time to time. My daughter used to say purple went with everything and wore it constantly. One day it simply disappeared from her wardrobe. I don't think she was even aware of it. Her interests and taste changed. Coming slowly and subtly, change is always interesting. This can happen in your garden.

White Flowering Annuals

*Ageratum**	*Lobularia** (alyssum)
*Antirrhinum** (snapdragon)	*Matthiola** (stock)
Callistephus (aster)	*Myosotis* (forget-me-not)
Centaurea (bachelor's button)	*Nicotiana**
Consolida orientalis (larkspur)	*Nigella* (love-in-a-mist)
Cosmos	*Pelargonium** (geranium)
*Dianthus** (pinks)	*Petunia**
Dimorphotheca (African daisy)	*Papaver* (poppy)
Dolichos lablab (hyacinth bean)	*Phlox**
Gyposophila (baby's breath)	*Scabiosa** (pincushion flower)
*Iberis** (candytuft)	*Tagetes** (marigold)
Impatiens	*Verbena**
*Ipomoea** (moonflower)	*Viola** (pansy)
Lobelia	*Zinnia*

*Fragrant flowers.

Opposite, from top: White cleomes and red salvias are a striking combination. Second photograph: This rainbow garden, designed by Rosalind Creasy, includes from top left: blue salvias, yellow and orange cosmos 'Bright Lights', red salvia, yellow marigolds, blue ageratums, and alyssum 'Royal Carpet'. Third photograph: White impatiens glow at dusk. Bottom: Spiky blue salvia contrasts with the flat, double form of yellow zinnias.

WINNING PLANT COMBINATIONS

No two gardens are alike, and the combinations of color, texture, and design are endless. Color is the single most impor- tant element holding partnerships together. To get you started in selecting your own combinations —of color, texture and designs— here are a few that work espe- cially well together.

Alyssums and Dahlberg daisies

Yellow, green, and white coleuses with red ivy geraniums

Lobelias and impatiens

Geraniums and alyssums

Blue ageratums and yellow marigolds

Yellow marigolds and blue periwinkles

Blue salvia, pink and white cleomes, and euphorbias

Purple ruffled basil, periwinkles, malvas, and cleomes

Scarlet celosias and blue salvias

CUTTING FLOWERS

Cutting flowers is one of a gardener's great pleasures. He can bring them into the home and arrange them for the living room, the dining room, the bedroom, wherever they will be enjoyed by family and friends.

An especially nice feature to keep in mind with cutting flowers is that the more you cut, the more flowers your annuals produce. The supply is self-perpetuating.

I also plant flowers among my vegetables for cutting purposes and these I relentlessly strip of blossoms, for our house and for giving to friends and neighbors. If you choose the latter location, you can lay the garden out in easily accessible rows and mulch with black plastic between the rows. If you don't like the appearance of the plastic, cover it with straw or grass. This is a strictly functional cutting garden.

When you begin planning the flowers you want to grow for cutting, include many that are fragrant. This will enhance your pleasure.

A cutting garden featuring dahlias and cosmos, among others, is beautiful as well as functional.

CONDITIONING CUT FLOWERS

There is a proper way to cut and condition flowers to prolong their life, often helping them live two weeks or longer. As a home gardener, you can prolong the life of flowers with a few simple procedures borrowed from professional florists. Don't just pick and cut. Use these guidelines:

The time to gather cut flowers is when the sun is low, in the morning or evening. Stems are apt to wilt quickly if cut in midday when the sun is hot and the plants are losing water. If you must cut in the middle of the day, carry a bucket of warm water and immerse the stems as quickly as you cut them.

Cut flower stems at an angle, with stems as long as possible without taking too many unopened buds. Buds are tomorrow's flowers. Make the cut with clean, sharp shears or a sharp knife. You don't want to crush or bruise the stems. If there are leaves at the bottom of the stem, remove them; if left on the stem under water, they will decay and smell unpleasant.

The most effective steps for prolonging the bloom of your cut flowers are those taken early. You want the plants to absorb as much water as possible, and you can sometimes double the life of cut flowers by plunging them in warm water (100 to 110 degrees Fahrenheit) as soon after they are picked as possible. Here the emphasis is on warm. It's easy to think the opposite: You splash your face with cold water to stimulate and wake up your senses, but with flowers the opposite holds. Warmth stimulates and cold slows down the action within the plants.

After cutting and immersing the flowers in warm water, place them in a cool place for a few hours to allow the stems to completely fill with water. The cool air and warm water combination conditions the flowers and extends their life as cut flowers.

Small packets of commercial preservatives are available. You can purchase them from florists and nurseries. They prolong the life of cut flowers and are used by professional florists and flower growers. The packets contain beneficial chemicals as follows:

1. Sugar, in a form that can be used by the plant for quick energy.
2. Bacteria inhibitors that prevent the stems from clogging.
3. Acidic compounds that lower the alkalinity of the water and impede the growth of microorganisms.
4. Metallic salts that help preserve the color of the flowers.
5. Respiratory inhibitors to lower the metabolic rate of the flowers.

Use the packets while conditioning the flowers and again later when arranging the flowers. They will keep your flowers healthy, blooming, and holding their heads high.

ANNUALS IN CONTAINERS

From top: Shade-loving annuals, from left to right: Coleuses, impatiens, and celosias; impatiens; petunias and morning glories. Second photograph: Impatiens and lobelias. Above left: Geraniums and blue lobelias. Above right: Sweet peas. Right: Vincas and polkadot plant 'Pink Splash'.

Annuals are naturals for growing in containers because of their long bloom time, wide assortment of colors, and relatively easy care. Containers can be as traditional as clay pots, wooden boxes, hanging pots, window boxes, and wheelbarrows, or as unconventional as old shoes, rubber tires, whiskey tubs, or an old rowboat. There are almost as many different kinds of containers for flowers as there are different kinds of annuals to grow in them.

Window boxes do double duty, overflowing with annuals that peek in your window, brightening your view while softening the exterior, adding color and charm. Pots of flowers on either side of your entrance greet your guests. Groups of containers on a terrace are a movable garden and an easy way to decorate. Containers that can be moved enable you to decorate different areas at different times. With so many possibilities, you are limited only by your imagination and the strength of your back.

One of the best features of container gardening is being able to move the flowers indoors before the first frost, thus bringing summer indoors and extending it well into fall and winter.

The same principles of design that work for a garden work for a container. It is best to limit the colors in a single container, however, to one or two depending on its size. If you would like more color in an area, it is better to plant more containers with different colors, for they can then be moved about where they will complement each other.

Foliage is important in a container garden. Ivies, artemisias, and coleuses, while they don't flower, can be a fitting backdrop that draws attention to the flowering plant or plants in the containers.

The larger containers will benefit from having plants that drape over the edges and even cascade down the sides to soften the effect of upright plants. The cascading plants give a container a finished, fuller look. Many ivies, lobelias, nasturtiums, and geraniums work well when planted this way. I have even had morning glories growing down the sides of a large pot or window box. They draw your attention, growing in an unexpected way.

Plant your container plants closer together than you would in a garden. With good soil, a deep pot, and weekly liquid fertilizing, you can grow many plants in a small area. An 8-inch hanging basket can hold between three and five plants, while a 10-inch hanging basket will hold five to seven plants. If you are filling your basket with rooted cuttings that are small, you can use more: three to five for a 6-inch pot, five to seven for an 8-inch pot, and seven to nine for a 10-inch pot.

USE A SUITABLE GROWING MEDIUM. Soil preparation is the most important factor when growing any plant. When you are planting a container garden, simply buy a specially formulated potting soil mix that provides balanced nutrients, fertilizer, and good drainage. These planting materials not only promote plant growth but are relatively light—an important plus for container gardening. Pots, boxes, and hanging baskets can be heavy to move around or suspend but are much easier to handle when weight is kept to a minimum. You should, however, put any large container in its permanent location before filling and planting.

If you're tempted to use garden soil in your containers because it is close at hand and costs nothing, think again. Garden soil is not sterile and contains weed seed, insects, and perhaps a fungus or two. Garden soil usually also lacks the many necessary nutrients for healthy growth, which are needed more than ever by plants growing in a container, where they are planted closer together than in the garden. Do yourself a favor and save time and aggravation later on by using a good prepared soil for your containers and replace it each year. Good potting soil is essential for containers and not very expensive.

The biggest disadvantage to a container garden is that potted plants dry out much faster than plants in a garden, and the roots are more exposed to heat and cold because they are above ground. Leaves are exposed to wind, and moisture is lost through transpiration. Fortunately, by using the latest garden products and technology, we can eliminate these problems. Soil additives are readily and cheaply available that, when

mixed with your planting medium, vastly increase water retention and slowly release water to plants over time as needed. The granules absorb many times their volume in water as they turn into a gel, and slowly and steadily release the water over time, which relieves you of frequent watering while protecting the plant from overwatering.

Overwatering is the number one cause of container plants' dying. When a plant is overwatered, the effects don't show until several days later, when the leaves yellow, rot, and fall off. Often it is too late to save the plant. To determine if a plant is too soggy, stick a finger into the soil. If pressing the soil brings water to the surface, the soil is soggy. If it is moist to the touch, it is perfect.

Here are some simple rules to help avoid overwatering:

1. Whenever possible, plant in a pot with a drainage hole in the bottom. This allows excess water to run off immediately.
2. Water thoroughly and allow the water to drain out the bottom of the pot. Never let water sit in a saucer under a plant.
3. When you have to use a pot without a drainage hole, fill the bottom of the pot (one to two inches) with gravel, broken pieces of a clay pot, pebbles, or other coarse material, before filling it with your planting medium. This way you are providing a place for the water to drain so the soil will not retain the water and drown the roots.
4. Never water without feeling the soil first to make sure it is dry to the touch. Most plants like to dry out between waterings.

Top left: Blue lobelias cascade prettily over the sides of this container, an unusual garden accent when placed on a column.

Top right: Blue lobelias and white geraniums brighten a lightly shaded terrace.

Center: An old carriage makes an unusual container for browallias.

Bottom: Window boxes of upright petunias are softened when draped with blue lantanas.

Morning glories and ivy trail over and down the sides of a large container.

Fragrant Annuals

Ageratum	Lobularia (alyssum)
Antirrhinum (snapdragon)	Matthiola (stock)
Calendula (pot marigold)	Nicotiana
Centaurea (bachelor's button)	Pelargonium (geranium)
Cleome	Petunia
Dianthus (pinks)	Phlox
Heliotrope	Scabiosa (pincushion flower)
Iberis (candytuft)	Tagetes (marigold)
Ipomoea (moonflower)	Verbena
Lathyrus (sweet pea)	Viola (pansy)

Care of Container Plants

1. Feed container plants about once a week with a water-soluble fertilizer, according to package directions. Since frequent watering washes nutrients out of the growing medium, it is necessary to apply fertilizer regularly and often.

2. By picking off faded flowers and seed pods, you will increase the number of flowers and extend the season of bloom for your plants. If your plant becomes leggy and loses its shape, pinch back the tips to encourage growth closer to the middle of the stems.

3. Check the undersides of the leaves of your plant for disease or insects each time you water. It is easier to control pests and disease when you catch them early. A diseased plant can easily be isolated from other plants. If the treatment requires spraying, the plant can be put in a plastic bag, or a dry cleaning bag, depending on its size. The fumes and spray can be contained around the plant. (Don't leave the bag on more than a few hours or you may kill the plants.)

4. To cut down on transpiration moisture loss, avoid placing the container in an exceptionally windy area. Also avoid hot areas that bake the containers and the soil.

THE ANNUAL PLANTING AND GROWING GUIDE

FROM THE BOTTOM UP: SOIL PREPARATION

The Burpee Company has been growing and packaging seeds for more than a century, and their early brochures carried the following advice: "As long as you have a sunny spot where the soil is rich and well drained, you can raise your favorite flowers and vegetables."

This advice from Burpee is still good. If you turn the soil over and add some peat moss or, even better, compost from your own pile, you'll do well. But today we strive for perfection. We want the hardiest deep green leaves, the sturdiest stems, the greatest number of blooms. These results come from the best soil, and the best soil needs proper preparation. Over the last century there have been great improvements, both scientific and practical, in our knowledge of soil that have helped us actually better soil conditions. The old saying, "Put a dollar plant in a ten-dollar hole, not a ten-dollar plant in a dollar hole," highlights the most important point to remember. Your garden can be only as good as your soil.

So when starting a garden, the greatest effort should be spent on improving the soil. A plant lives and breathes. It needs food, water, and air.

Ideal soil has good drainage, good water retention and good nutrients. It should hold just enough water to meet the needs of the plant, but not so much as to force the air out of the soil and deprive the plant of one of its basic needs.

Squeeze a handful of wet soil between your fingers. If it holds a tight shape, you have clay. If it falls through your fingers, you have sand. If it shows the imprint of your fingers and slowly disintegrates as you open your hand, your soil has the right texture. This is the test that farmers have used for centuries.

Usually the best soil in any garden lies in the top few inches, the top soil. This is where you find plant roots, worms, and organic material. Top soil is usually darker in color, lighter in weight, easier to dig, and more nutritious than subsoil.

When you dig straight down, you'll see that the color of the soil changes. There are layers, and the best is uppermost.

For an annual garden it is important to prepare the ground at least 8 inches deep, deeper if your soil is clay and your area has heavy rainfall.

Above left: Clay soil
Above right: Loamy soil
Left: Sandy soil

Soil can be classified under three categories:

CLAY: *The material from which bricks and pottery are made. A solid mass that retains water, is slow to dry out and, when it does, becomes rock-hard.*

SAND: *What we find on beaches. If you've ever watched a wave roll over the sand, you've noticed how the color of the sand changes as the water drenches it but then moves rapidly through it, leaving it nearly dry before your eyes. Living in sand, a plant has to be pretty quick to get a drink. Also, nutrients and fertilizer will leach out and have to be replaced more often than in heavier soil.*

LOAM: *The ideal we strive for. Loam is a combination of sand and/or clay with organic matter. Nature's example of perfect soil texture is the black, rich soil of a forest floor, where leaves and pine needles have collected and decomposed for years, replenishing that soil with nutrients and allowing good drainage while retaining moisture. Loam also provides a good home for bacteria and worms, which are constantly at work, burrowing and feeding on fallen leaves and dead vegetable matter, to further aerate and improve the texture of the soil.*

STEPS FOR SOIL PREPARATION

Step One

After you have chosen a garden location, remove any vegetation or turf and turn the soil over, loosening it and breaking up any clumps. The best tool is a shovel, a digging fork, a spade, or a rototiller. All break up the ground effectively and are easy to work with. If digging by hand, turn the topmost soil over to the depth of the shovel and eliminate the lumps by chopping with the fork or spade. If you use a rototiller, go back and forth over the area several times. Each time the rototiller covers the same patch, the blades will reach a little deeper into the soil. When the soil has been thoroughly turned, rake the surface smooth.

Step Two

Every soil benefits from a yearly addition of compost or peat moss. Peat moss absorbs twenty times its weight in water. Adding it is a way of improving the texture of the soil and increasing its absorbency. The amount needed depends on the condition of the soil. Generally, laying three inches of peat moss or compost on top of the soil, adding a sprinkling of lime (to compensate for the acidity of the compost) and then rototilling or digging in to a depth of 8 inches will prepare most soils.

If your soil is very sandy or solid clay, it must be improved before planting. Raise your bed a few inches above the previous level by adding peat moss or compost and top soil, working it into the existing soil, then mounding your soil several inches high. Clay soils will then drain better and sandy soils will have more absorbency.

Step Three

Most annuals prefer slightly acid conditions but are tolerant of some variation toward either acidity or alkalinity. The only way to know exactly how much lime or fertilizer your garden needs is to have a soil test made through your local County Agricultural Agent or your local nursery, by making a test yourself with an inexpensive soil kit, or by using a slightly more costly pH meter. The home test kit and pH meter are available from gardening catalogs and at most local gardening centers.

The condition of the soil is measured on a scale of acidity that runs from 1 to 14. It is referred to as the pH scale. A pH reading tells the gardener whether his soil is acid (1 to 6.5), neutral (6.5 to 7.5), or alkaline (7.5 through 14). Most annuals like the soil just a little left of center, about 6.5, although anywhere between 6 and 7 will bring good results. Readings at either extreme indicate conditions under which the nutrients in the soil are less available to the plants and the plants are deprived of food. When taking a soil sample or reading, be sure to take more than one, from different areas of the garden. Often soil differs from one spot to another.

Compost is the ideal additive for soil as it not only conditions the soil, but adds nutrients to help plants thrive.

If pH readings suggest that your soil needs sweetening to move the reading up the scale toward 6.5, you may need to add agricultural lime (preferably, ground limestone). This is available from garden supply and hardware stores. Directions for use are explained on the packaging, but as a general rule, 5 pounds will raise the unit reading per 100 square feet one point on the pH scale. The best time to add lime to the soil is in the fall; it will have all winter long to break down and mix in thoroughly.

If your pH reading is higher than 7, you need to increase the acidity of your soil. A reading just slightly above 7 can be remedied by the addition of peat moss or leaf or pine needle compost. They will add some acid to the soil, but also will help the soil retain water and nutrients.

However, if your reading goes above 7.5, you will need iron sulfate. Figure on a rate of 3 pounds per 100 square feet, which will lower the pH count about one unit. Iron sulfate too is available at your garden center or local hardware store. Complete instructions will be on the package. This conditioner should also be applied in the fall, for it takes time to mix properly with the soil.

Step Four

Step four is the final one in good soil preparation. It involves adding food for the plants to thrive on.

Food, or fertilizer, is made up of three ingredients: nitrogen, phosphorous, and potassium. The combination is referred to by their chemical symbols, NPK.

Nitrogen promotes vegetative growth, making the plants lush and green. Excess nitrogen will work at the expense of the blossoms. Your plants will be strong, the green leaves dark and beautiful, but the blossoms few. In many areas of the country, excess nitrogen is seeping deep into the earth and polluting our drinking water. Use nitrogen CAUTIOUSLY and follow the instructions on the package.

Phosphorous gives plants energy and vitality, and contributes to root growth and healthy flowers.

Potassium also promotes strong plant growth, which in turn helps plants become disease-resistant and healthier.

All three can be applied through organic fertilizers (compost or manure) or in a more controlled fashion by chemical fertilizers available at your garden supply house and most hardware stores. Commercial fertilizers come in granular forms that break down quickly, or in slow-release formulas that break down slowly and stay in the soil longer. Liquid fertilizers are also available; they reach the plants more quickly but need to be used more often than dry fertilizers.

Each package of fertilizer is coded with three numbers which give the amount, in percentages, of the three chemical ingredients in the mixture. Thus, 5–10–5 means the fertilizer has 5 percent nitrogen, 10 percent phosphorus, and 5 percent potassium. The remainder of the mixture is a neutral ingredient to help distribute the chemicals evenly. The 5–10–5 combination is the best all-around fertilizer for annuals. Apply it evenly and work it into your soil at least a week before planting time. Then apply once more just as the plants begin to flower.

(Caution: Lawn fertilizers are very high in nitrogen and should not be used without a soil test to see if one is needed. They should never be used on flowering plants.)

COMPOST

Composting is as easy as it is important for the successful garden. Compost is broken down organic matter and, once the gardener gets compost properly started, he or she simply waits for Nature to do her job. Starting a good compost heap can be as uncomplicated as saving fall leaves in a pile behind the garage. An alternative is to set up a compost bin, homemade or purchased, and alternate layers of organic matter with layers of soil, lime, and fertilizer.

Pick the method that suits you depending on the time and money you have to spend, and the size of your garden. The important thing is to use compost for the health of your plants. Healthy soil grows healthy plants. Adding compost to your garden will improve the soil structure, water-holding capacity and aeration of the soil, and contribute needed nutrients.

Organic material is all around you: grass cuttings, leaves, tea

leaves, vegetable peelings, and small twigs.

You can buy durable compost bins with thermally insulated walls to trap solar heat and ventilation slots to provide aeration and prevent odors. They also have sliding doors at the bottom for easy access to the compost.

To hasten decomposition and add more nutrients, alternate layers of organic material (4 to 6 inches thick) with 1 inch of soil, and a thin covering of lime (just enough to look like a dusting of snow). The soil is added to introduce microorganisms and worms that will speed up the breakdown of the soil and the lime is to offset the acidity of the leaves and other material. With grass clippings, composting takes between 10 and 30 days, while autumn leaves compost in about 60 to 90 days. Both decompose to a fine, velvety brown soil. During the winter season when the compost freezes, the process slows down. Chopping up the leaves with a lawn mower or chipper will hasten the composting.

The compost pile contains organic matter which includes microorganisms (bacteria) and macroorganisms (earthworms, beneficial nematodes, and other insects). As long as oxygen is present, the fast-acting aerobic bacteria decompose materials most rapidly, breaking them down into beneficial plant food. Turn the compost pile often to reactivate the oxygen-consuming organisms and speed things up. When oxygen is used up, composting continues, but more slowly.

While the compost is breaking down, the temperature in the center of the compost pile can rise to between 150 and 170 degrees Fahrenheit. Heat is good, but should not be allowed to rise so high that it destroys the beneficial earthworms or dries everything out, for the compost will then lose some of its soil-improving abilities. To control the temperature, water the pile down every week or two, unless there is plenty of rain.

Add compost to your soil at least once a year. The continuous and ongoing decomposition of compost requires that it be replenished; as it breaks down, it loses its nutrients and ability to hold water. If your soil is loose and crumbly, even in midsummer, you know you have good tilth (soil condition).

It sounds like more work than it is. Nature does most of the work while the gardener waits.

What to put in the compost pile—

Remember that the smaller the pieces are, the faster they will decompose:

shredded or whole fall leaves (first drag a lawn mower back and forth over leaves to shred, or use a leaf shredder)
shredded bark (you'll need a wood chipper for this)
shredded twigs
fresh vegetable and fruit peelings
grass cuttings
tea leaves
coffee grounds
well-rotted horse or cow manure
eggshells
cut flowers
salt hay*
pine needles

What not to put in the compost pile:

cooked food
weeds with seed pods
raw fish and animal remains (good compost, but they attract mice and other small animals)
diseased plants (the disease will spread)
any plant material that has been treated with a herbicide or pesticide within the past three weeks

*This is made from wild grass (sold at nurseries) grown in salt water. Unlike common hay, salt hay does not contain seeds.

Top left: This compost starter bin is easy to make from four 4-foot posts, set in a square or rectangle, wrapped in chicken wire. If the chicken wire is secured loosely on the fourth side, the bin can be opened easily for removal of compost or for working the compost pile.

SEEDS

A seed is a miraculous growth machine, surrounded by enough food to sustain it until it can put down roots to gather nourishment from the soil and put up a stem and leaves to gather more nourishment from the sun. A seed is unbelievably sturdy and self-sufficient.

The Quality of Seeds

Hybrid seeds come from parent plants carefully selected and crossed by breeders. They must be produced each year under scientifically controlled conditions, for the first generation seed of a hybrid reverts to a weaker replica of one of the parent plants. For this reason, hybrids must be cross-pollinated carefully from the same parents each year. Some hybrids are individually hand-pollinated in the fields, one reason they are more expensive for the home gardener. The hybrids are bred to be vigorous and disease-resistant. Seedsmen look to enhance variety in height and color, and to produce prolific blooming flowers that last from spring until the first frost. The result for today's gardener is more beautiful flowers, with lusher foliage and hardier growing qualities. To find these varieties, look for the word "hybrid" in the flower name printed on the seed packet.

Planting Your Seeds

When you're ready to plant, consider seed size. Large seeds can easily be transferred to your hand and placed one at a time to the depth and at the distance advised on the packages. Don't crowd plants, as crowding weakens them and results in fewer flowers. Roots need room to spread.

It is more difficult to control the planting of tiny seeds. One way to plant them is to fold a piece of paper in half, empty your seeds onto it, and slowly let them fall out of the crease onto their seed bed. You can also mix the tiny seeds with sand and then spread them, but you'll need more sand than seed to be successful. This method is good for direct sowing in the garden. If the seeds are large enough, plant them by hand, one at a time, at the proper distance specified on the back of the seed packet; if small, pour them into your hand and brush a few at a time to where you want them.

The back of the seed package will tell you the proper depth at which to plant the seeds. A general rule is two to four times their diameter for larger seeds, and on the surface—barely covered—if they are tiny. The tiniest will find crevasses to enter and will need no covering at all. But very tiny seeds should be started indoors where they will be protected from wind, heavy rains, and birds.

Starting Seeds Indoors

Although I enjoy winter, it invariably lasts too long for me and I am always impatient for the arrival of spring. Starting seeds indoors lets me get my hands dirty sooner and helps

me realize my garden dreams earlier too. By starting indoors varieties that take several months to bloom, you can extend by weeks the length of time the flowers bloom in the garden before frost. Seedlings transplanted into the warming, frost-free garden soil will flower much faster than if they had been planted directly at a later date. By starting them indoors, you get the seedlings through the early stages of four to six weeks and they develop the stems and leaves which support the blooms in a protected, controlled environment, away from heavy rain, strong wind, and substantial fluctuations in temperature. Another important advantage is that I have a wider choice of flowers from seed, many unusual and not available as plants from nurseries.

But again, timing is important. If the seedlings will be

This hybrid marigold is much more attractive and vigorous than either of its parents, shown above it to the left and right.

ready to plant outside in six weeks, it's important to plant the seeds indoors about six weeks before the last frost leaves your area. If you plant seeds too early, they will grow weak and spindly before you can plant them in a frost-free garden.

Planting seeds indoors provides perfect conditions away from the elements and allows you to capture extra weeks of flowering time as the flowers bloom soon after the seedlings are set out.

There are many different kinds of equipment for seed starting. It is important to understand how a seed grows and what is necessary for its growth. Not all seeds have the same requirements. "Plant Portraits," page 37, or your seed pack will tell you the requirements specific to the variety. After reading the information you can easily decide which equipment and method of growing will suit you best.

SEED TIPS

1. *Air and water:* All seeds need air and moisture to germinate. If they are too wet, sitting in a puddle or soggy soil, they are deprived of air and will rot instead of germinate. Keep them damp, but not soaking wet.

2. *Temperature:* Every seed variety germinates best at a certain temperature. Most annual seeds like a temperature between 65 and 80 degrees Fahrenheit. However, some seeds prefer cooler temperatures. It is best to check each seed variety for the preferable temperature.

3. *Light or dark:* Most seeds germinate best in the dark (that is one reason we usually bury them). It is important to be aware of those seeds that require light—impatiens, begonias, and petunias—because they will not germinate without it. Set them in a sunny window or keep them under grow lights. For the seeds that require darkness, the planting depth is important. Read your seed packet and plant accurately.

4. *Days to germination:* This will tell you approximately how many days before you can see your seed sprouting. When a seed has sprouted, its requirements change. If it needed dark to germinate, it now needs light to grow. While germinating it has supplied its own food; now it needs to be fed by the sun, soil, and moisture.

5. *Transplanting:* Some annuals do not like to be moved. If transplanted they will go into shock and temporarily stop growing or even die. Poppies, sweet peas, and larkspurs are examples, but check each variety you plan to transplant, in "Plant Portraits," page 37, or on your seed packs.

The earliest new selections Burpee introduced, in the 1880s, were the 'Defiance pansy,' and the 'Defiance petunia'. They were so named because they defied nature and bloomed more than a pansy or petunia was expected to at that time.

MAINTENANCE

Maintenance is an act of love for a gardener not unlike raising children. A gardener must teach his plants manners and keep them from being unruly; he must enforce discipline and nurture them through ill-health.

Look on gardening as a celebration of life, not drudgery. Gardening, for the most part, is a pleasurable, uniquely rewarding experience. To call gardening a form of maintenance lumps it together with jobs like washing the dishes, taking out the garbage, or cleaning out the garage. Gardening should be thought of as an activity similar to golf or tennis that requires effort to perfect, but rewards the energy expended with a special sense of accomplishment. The real reward of gardening is in the doing, being close to nature, nurturing and watching flowers grow and their beauty shine forth. A gardener is closely connected with nature, the seasons, and the renewal of life. This was aptly expressed by Thomas Jefferson after a lifetime of gardening: "Though an old man, I am but a young gardener."

A gardener today has at his disposal the benefit of centuries of garden knowledge as well as new products that save time and energy, and ward off disappointment. Gardening has never been an exact science. We all learn by trial and error. What works well in one garden might be slightly different in another. Every gardener has his or her own tricks, tips, and style. Just as no two gardens are alike, neither are the methods of any two gardeners.

Watering

Many plants are lost and much water wasted due to improper watering methods. During the growing season, plants require, on the average, one inch of rainfall per week. Furthermore, this need continues until the garden freezes in winter. Nature may provide rainfall but if not, the gardener must provide water instead.

The way you water is very important. Too much overhead watering can create an environment for insects and disease. Waving a hose around to sprinkle a garden is not the way to do it either. Frequent and shallow waterings are useless and can cause damage by encouraging formation of roots too near the surface. When you water, it should be done thoroughly, supplying enough water to penetrate the soil to a depth of at least six inches. At least one inch of water at each application is optimum. This may take three to four hours or more, depending on the delivery capacity of your watering equipment.

You can measure the amount of rainfall or water you are putting on the garden by using a rain gauge. A homemade rain gauge won't give an accurate reading. One inch of rain collected in a 10½-ounce soup can may read two to three inches in a rain gauge. A rain gauge can be purchased inexpensively at most nurseries or through garden catalogs.

Wherever and whenever possible, soaking rather than spraying equipment should be used. Soakers or drippers deliver water most effectively, wasting little to evaporation or runoff, and avoiding water on the foliage, which can sometimes cause problems.

How often to water during a period of drought is largely determined by the soil type. On average, loam soils, once every ten days or so should suffice for established plantings. Sandy soils drain faster, so once every week may be necessary, while clay soils retain moisture better and probably need to be irrigated only every two weeks. But remember, when you water, deliver at least one inch.

Good water is becoming scarce and more precious. Conserve water by using it correctly!

Feeding

Annuals require feeding to supply the high amounts of energy and nutrients required to produce flowers continuously. Growing plants deplete the soil of nitrogen, phosphates, and potash as well as other minor, but necessary, trace elements. Each plant's needs are individual, so we have to be careful not to starve or overfeed them. There are even plants, like nasturtium, that prefer "infertile" conditions (there is a plant for every place) but these are the exceptions.

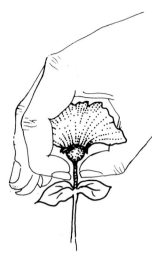

Remove spent blossoms to prolong bloom and prevent the formation of seeds. That way, flowers devote more of their energy to blooming.

If you are adding well-rotted compost or manure to your garden yearly, chemical fertilizers are unnecessary. If not, work a slow-release granular fertilizer into the soil in spring or fall. This is all that is usually necessary. For an added boost, you can liquid-fertilize when transplanting and again right before flower buds open, but this is optional. A liquid fertilizer, if watered-in deeply, goes directly to the plant roots and is easier for the plant to absorb. However, it doesn't stay in the soil long.

If your plants appear to be growing unusually slowly or come under attack by pests or diseases, a quicker method of absorption is to use a liquid foliage feed. Use any all-purpose liquid fertilizer at half-strength and spray it directly on the leaves, where it is absorbed immediately. The plant leaves can send the nutrition to the roots for added vigor.

Deadheading

An annual's purpose in life is to perpetuate its species by developing a profusion of seeds. To accomplish this, it must first produce flowers. You can keep annuals in flower longer by deadheading (pinching off the flower blossoms) before they start forming seed.

TIPS FOR GARDENING SUCCESS IN DROUGHT

1. **Mulch to conserve water.** Mulching conserves moisture in the soil by reducing the rate of evaporation. Lay on the mulches when the soil is moist, because ground mulched when the soil is dry is apt to stay dry if rainfall is sparse.
2. **Use shade to advantage.** Moisture evaporates more slowly in shaded soil than in sun.
3. **Space plants closely.** Space plants and rows so the leaves of mature plants just overlap. This will shade the ground to reduce moisture loss and eliminate weed competition.

4. **Weed regularly.** Weeds compete with flowers for every drop of water, and often the stronger, deep-rooted weeds win the competition! Remove weeds as soon as they show themselves in your garden.
5. **Water deeply, not often.** Water in the early morning with soil-soaking hoses that allow water to drip slowly into the ground, and place the hoses quite close to your plants. Or set your garden hose, nozzle removed, directly on the ground to irrigate one part of your garden at a time. Let the water run slowly for as long as necessary to soak deeply into the soil. A deep soaking is needed only every ten to fourteen days, unless your plants show signs of wilting from insufficient moisture. The deeper soaking will encourage deep-rooted plants, which survive drought better than shallow-rooted ones. Oscillating-type lawn sprinklers throw water where you may not need it and allow much more evaporation than other watering methods.

PROPAGATION THROUGH CUTTINGS

Some annuals that are slow to grow from seed are readily propagated through cuttings. In the fall, before your annuals are killed by frost, you can take cuttings to grow over the winter and plant outside again in the spring, or to use as house plants. Some annuals root so easily that they can be started in a glass of water. This is not, however, a good way to grow a healthy root because later your cutting might have trouble adjusting to soil, and you can't grow a plant in water alone.

To grow from cuttings:

1. Cut a 3- to 4-inch piece of a new tender stem, making sure to cut ½ inch below a node, the place where two or more branches or leaves come together. This is essential. The cutting will then have sufficient food reserves within its tissues to sustain it until roots have been produced.

2. Leave two or three leaves, to prevent wilting, and to promote rooting for the plant. More than three leaves makes it hard for the stem to stay alive without roots. Remove any flowers or flower buds to prevent them from sapping the stem's energy. Most cuttings benefit from being dipped in a rooting hormone (for geraniums it is unnecessary.) The rooting hormone helps speed the growth of healthy new roots.

3. Fill a tray or a cup with a moist, not soggy, rooting medium (sand and vermiculite are two rooting media.) Make a hole in the medium with a pencil. This hole should be wider than the stem of the cutting, so as not to damage the stem or rub off any of the hormone powder when it is placed in the medium. Stand the stem up in the hole and gently push the rooting medium around it. Place the node under the medium; this is where the roots will form.

4. Cover with clear plastic or put in a plastic bag and place in a warm spot. This will keep the atmosphere around the cutting moist. Rooting is promoted by moisture and warmth, particularly bottom heat. Set the cutting top of a refrigerator or a warm—not hot—radiator, or under a cold frame in partial, not full, sun.

5. Different plants root at different speeds. Top growth starts after the roots have developed. Don't worry if you don't see new leaves and stems forming for several months; as long as your stems are healthy they are fine. If you see rot or mildew, separate the stem from other cuttings and discard.

Make a cut about ½ inch below a node.

Gently firm the rooting medium around the stem.

A clear plastic covering ensures a moister environment for the cutting.

PLANT PORTRAITS

The more than seventy plants that follow were selected for their popularity, and ability to bloom from seed and flower their first season. Not all are "annuals" in strict horticultural terms, but all "behave" like annuals, are easy to grow, and offer a wide range of color and a long period of bloom. Through them, you will learn the joy of gardening while being assured of success.

Flower favorites, like fashion styles, change. In the words of a nineteenth-century garden writer, "Today we are at the feet of a Dahlia; tomorrow there is no beauty like a Pansy, and both are presently deserted for a Cineraria." The preferences are in the eye of the beholder and in our skill in growing the flowers we choose.

As a gardener myself, I can assure you that your interest in unusual plants will broaden. Still, many of the first annuals you ever plant will continue to be your favorites. It is one of the pleasures of annual gardening to have so many varieties to choose from each year. New flowers continue to arrive, from all over the world and through our own breeders and researchers. You can plan a new garden every year or you can continue using the same annuals in different ways, or you can mix some new plants in with the old acquaintances. Experiment and enjoy your discoveries.

As you look through the "Plant Portraits," don't be dismayed or confused by the alphabetical listing of annuals under the botanical (Latin) names. You'll find this avoids confusion and ensures the plant names are scientifically correct. Our catalogs from one hundred years ago listed flowers by the same names. This system of nomenclature, founded by the Swedish botanist Carolus Linnaeus, gives every plant two names: genus, followed by species. The genus (the first word), is the name of a group that shares certain characteristics. Every genus is broken down further into numerous species (the second word). Members of the same species share qualities too, but qualities of lesser importance.

We admit, as Celia Thaxter (an American garden writer at the turn of the century) says, "*Eschscholzia* is an ugly name for a most lovely flower. California poppy is much better." However, many different flowers grown in different parts of the country have the same common name. A daisy is and is not a daisy; there are hundreds of flowers commonly called daisies from many different families of plants. Using botanical names is the one way to be sure of conveying the correct cultural information. To make life simpler, common names are cross-referenced throughout this book so you can readily find what you are looking for.

The "Plant Portraits" that follow do not tell you which annuals grow best in which zone, and for good reason. If the proper conditions are met, each of these annuals can grow in every region of the country. In southern gardens, annuals that love cool nights can be grown as spring-blooming flowers rather than in summer when the nights are too hot. In Maine, flowers that require a long growing time before bloom can be started earlier indoors, then transplanted outside to bring you blossoms throughout Maine's short growing season. Certainly some

Impatiens and hosta bloom side by side in the summer at the edge of a wood, covering a spot where tulips and daffodils bloomed in the spring. The soft transition from one shade to another leads your eye through the garden.

annuals are not as easily grown in areas that don't have the ideal conditions they love, but most are somewhat adaptable and with loving care will reward the gardener. So you have many choices to make. However, if you are a new gardener or a gardener with limited time, choose the annuals that thrive in your area with little care.

PLANT PORTRAIT KEY

Here is a guide to the symbols and terms used throughout this section.

Latin name of the annual is in boldface italic type.

Phonetic pronunciation of the Latin name is in parentheses.

Common name of the annual is in boldface type.

The average hours of sun needed per day is indicated by symbols. The first symbol is what the annual prefers, but the plant is adaptable to all conditions listed.

○ *Sun*—Six hours or more of direct sunlight per day.

◐ *Part shade*—Three to six hours of direct sunlight per day.

● *Shade*—Two hours or less of direct sunlight.

Symbols for:

    ◖ *Drought-resistant*

    ✳ *Heat lover*

    ✳ *Cool-weather annual*

    ◗ *Long-lasting cut flower*

    ❀ *Long bloomer—three months or longer*

Grade of difficulty—Annuals that take the least amount of care are identified as "easy." These plants are a good choice for beginning gardeners or gardeners with little time.

T—Tender annuals, plants that are killed by the first frost.

HH—Half-hardy annuals, annuals that can survive several frosts but will be killed by prolonged freezing.

H—Hardy annuals, like HH annuals except that they produce seedlings that will survive freezing weather.

Native American—plants that were growing on the American continent when the pilgrims arrived. Some, like the marigold, were only found here; others are similar to varieties grown elsewhere.

Heights are for normal growth, but annuals with very fertile soil and a longer growing season could grow taller. Conversely, with poor growing conditions, the plant could be shorter. The term "dwarf" can be deceiving, as it means "dwarf" only compared to its own species. Dwarf for a cosmos is three feet, while dwarf for an aster is six inches.

Cultural Information explains plants' preferences and when it's time to plant them. Some annuals should only be direct sown where they are to grow. For these varieties, no information is given on when to start indoors. Temperatures given for germination and growth are the optimum for growth indoors.

Days to Bloom guides you when to plant. Depending on heat, rain, sunshine, soil and region of the country, the number of days will vary. Entries for plants grown primarily for their foliage list the days needed to grow to a full plant with showy foliage.

Recommended Cultivars: We have recommended particular varieties or cultivars of annuals when there are many choices available, to help you understand the differences among cultivars and to inform you about exceptional ones.

Abutilon hybridum (ab-YEW-til-on HIB-rid-um) **flowering maple,** HH, Native American from the tropics, easy. ✿ ○ ◐

Height: 18 inches to 3 feet and up if wintered over indoors or grown in the South.

Colors: Apricot, salmon, white, yellow, purple.

Characteristics: Abutilons are grown mostly as houseplants, but are an unusual and striking addition to beds and borders in semishady areas. The plant is distinguished by light green, very soft, maple-leaf-shaped leaves (from which it gets its common name), bushy habit, and drooping trumpet- or bell-shaped flowers, 1½ to 2½ inches wide. In southern climates they can live and bloom for years, masquerading as flowering shrubs.

First-year plants are good in window boxes as the bottom branches, heavy with flowers, cascade over the edges of the containers.

Cultural Information: Abutilons like a moist, fertile soil and prefer protection from strong afternoon sun. Plant them in a soil rich in organic matter and keep them well-watered for the best results. A 2- to 3-inch layer of mulch around the base of each plant will help keep moisture from evaporating, and the plants will need less frequent watering. If you are growing them as houseplants, fertilize biweekly with an application of liquid fertilizer and mist regularly to maintain a moist atmosphere; this helps keep lower leaves from falling off. (If your plants are at the back of the border, the plants in front of them will hide the lower leaves and it won't matter if they fall off.) You can bring some in from the garden to winter over as houseplants, replanting them in the garden the following spring. For convenience and to keep from disturbing the roots, you can plant them, pot and all, directly in the garden. If you do this, follow up by cutting the side shoots back in March to within two or three buds of the base (removing the previous summer's growth and the old, weak growth). If the plant is several years old, shorten the previous year's growth by half. It is best to repot to a larger size, as the plant becomes rootbound. Keep warm and moist, 55 to 60 degrees Fahrenheit, and repot when fresh growth begins. In the first season, plants grown from seed will reach approximately 19 inches by summer's end. New plants can easily be made from cuttings. In a garden, space approximately 12 inches apart.

Days to germinate: 21 to 28; Germination temperature: 70 to 80 degrees Fahrenheit; Days to bloom: 105; Growth temperature: not below 50 degrees Fahrenheit: Weeks to start indoors: 8 to 10.

Uses: Middle or back of border, houseplant, window box, container, hanging basket.

African daisy; see ***Dimorphotheca***

Ageratum houstonianum (aj-er-AY-tum hew-stōn-ee-AH-num) **floss flower,** HH, Native American from Mexico, easy. ✺ ✿ ○ ◐

Height: 5 to 9 inches for dwarf varieties, 24 to 30 inches for tall varieties.

Colors: White, pinks, blues, purples.

Characteristics: Originally from Mexico and Central America, ageratums perform naturally in hot summer weather as long as they are well watered. The range of blue colors, from soft, clear blues, to powder blues and rich dark blue make ageratums very popular annuals.

There are dwarf, compact and tall, upright varieties. The compact varieties form mounds (twice as wide as they are high) of fuzzy, tufted blossoms that bloom from early summer to fall. They make a very showy edging,

Top: Abutilon hybridum
Above: Ageratum houstonianum 'Blue Danube Hybrid'

Amaranthus tricolor
'Splendens Perfecta'

defining a flower bed, and can be planted as a scallop or alternated with other dwarf edging plants such as alyssum for an interesting garden edging.

As the small flowers fade, they turn brown and can make the plant look messy. From time to time, deadhead the exhausted flowers; this also prolongs the blooming period. Plants can be dug up in the fall and brought indoors as houseplants for fall bloom.

'Blue Danube' and 'Pink Powderpuffs' are good dwarf varieties, depending on the color you prefer. For a tall variety, try 'Blue Horizon' which also makes a good cut flower.

Cultural Information: Ageratums prefer rich, well-watered soil. To grow from seed, press lightly into a planting formula (do not cover the seed) and keep evenly moist, not soggy.

The young plants are very tender and initial growth is slow. Right after transplanting into the garden is a good time to pinch back to induce bushiness. Ageratums can be propagated from cuttings but most are grown from seed. In the West Coast area where winters are mild, seed can be planted in late summer for fall bloom. Space dwarf varieties 6 inches apart, tall varieties 12 inches.

Days to germinate: 5 to 10; Germination temperature: 70 to 80 degrees Fahrenheit; Growth temperature: 60 to 65 degrees Fahrenheit; Days to bloom: 60 to 90; Weeks to start indoors: 6 to 10.
Uses: Houseplant, edging, cutting, rock garden, window box.

Alyssum; see *Lobularia*

Amaranthus (am-a-RAN-thus)
summer poinsettia, HH, easy.
🌢 ❀ ○

Height: 12 to 15 inches for dwarf varieties, 3 to 5 feet for tall varieties.
Colors: Reds, yellow, green, tricolor.
Characteristics: Amaranths are old-fashioned annuals prized as the parting gift of autumn. They were brought to America by early settlers, who grew them as medicinal herbs in the mistaken belief that their red leaves would stop bleeding. They were transported from their native India to England and then to America.

Their spectacular autumn-colored foliage attracts attention even from a distance. They are so pretty, they deserve to be more widely grown. Their bold colors need to be combined carefully with other plants. They are best used as accents, temporary shrubs, hedges, or as background for flowering plants, combining the colors of the sunset: red, orange, and yellow. They are quick-growing, varied in size, and long-enduring.

Their name, adapted from Greek, means "unfading [or] never fading flower." There are many different species within this genus. *Amaranthus caudatus,* the tassel-types (love-lies-bleeding, kiss-me-over-the-garden-gate), has tassels that last 6 to 8 weeks. The tassels are usually red, but can be white, a foot or more long, and droop over the leaves, hence the common name. The tassels can be cut and air-dried, retaining their bright color for winter bouquets. Instead of hanging them to dry, arrange them drooping in a vase; dried that way, they'll have a more natural look. *Amaranthus tricolor* (Joseph's coat) has bright crimson-scarlet and gold upper leaves and chocolate, yellow, and green lower leaves. This variety makes a colorful houseplant. So does 'Illumination' with upper leaves bright rosy red, topped with gold and lower leaves green and chocolate.

Cultural Information: Amaranths have better leaf color in poorer soil and dry-to-average moisture. They are fast-growing and can be direct sown after all danger of frost is past and the soil is warm, or they can be started indoors. When transplanting, be careful not to disturb the roots, as this slows growth. It is best to transplant after night temperatures stay above 50 degrees Fahrenheit. The smaller varieties can be spaced 18 inches apart, while taller varieties need two to three feet, depending on soil fertility and heat.

Days to germinate: 14 to 21; Germination temperature: 65 to 75 degrees Fahrenheit; Growth temperature: 70+ degrees Fahrenheit; Days to bloom: 65; Weeks to start indoors: 8 to 10.
Uses: Back of the border, accent, hedge, houseplant.

Antirrhinum majus (an-ti-RY-num MAH-yus) **snapdragon,** HH, easy. 🌑 ❀ ○ ◐
Height: 8 inches for dwarf varieties, 18 to 36 inches for intermediate to tall varieties.
Colors: White, scarlet, rose, crimson, pinks, yellows, orange, bicolors.
Characteristics: Softly colored, old-fashioned favorites for the garden. Some varieties are slightly fragrant. Snapdragons get their name from their blossoms, which resemble open mouths; if gently squeezed where they hinge, they snap open and shut, making them a favorite with children of all ages. Some of the newer varieties have flared, open faces, others are double-faced.

Plants bloom heavily in early summer and, if faded spikes are cut off, will continue all summer long, but with smaller flower stalks and fewer blooms. Flowers begin to open from the bottom of the stem and move up, so the spikes remain attractive even when the bottom flowers are past. Commercial flower growers cut snapdragons when the florets on the lower third of the stem are open. The other florets will continue to develop and open after picking if given light. If floral preservative is added, the blooms can last for as long as three weeks in water.

Snapdragons are perennials in frost-free areas and can bloom with light frost in northern climates. In mild climates, plants bloom from early winter until summer.

'Floral Carpet' is a good dwarf, 'Cinderella' is a good intermediate, and 'Topper' is a good choice for a tall variety; all are handsome and hardy. 'Butterfly' is the most popular double-flowering variety.
Cultural Information: Snapdragons do not like heavy soils, as their roots are very fine. If planting in heavy soil, add lots of compost. Best in cool weather, moderately rich soil, in sun or partial shade. They need light to germinate. The seeds are small and best started indoors.

Judicious watering is very important in snapdragon culture. Overwatering, especially during early growth, can produce soft, weak growth and induce root rot.

Rust can be a problem for snapdragons. It is best to grow rust-resistant varieties. Rust is easily recognized by the brown, dusty spots on the undersides of leaves and stems. Give plants room for good air circulation.

Tall varieties might need staking. Space 8 to 12 inches, depending on varieties.
Days to germinate: 8 to 14; Germination temperature: 65 to 75 degrees Fahrenheit; Growth temperature: 65 degrees Fahrenheit; Days to bloom: 53 to 65; Weeks before last frost to start indoors: 12.
Uses: Edging, border, cutting.

Aster; see *Callistephus*

Baby's breath; see *Gypsophila*

Bachelor's button; see *Centaurea*

Beefsteak plant; see *Perilla*

Begonia × semperflorens (be-GO-nee-a sem-per-FLO-renz) **fibrous begonia, wax begonia,** HH and *Begonia × tuberhybrida* (be-GO-nee-a too-ber-HI-bri-da) **tuberous begonia,**

Above: Begonia × tuberhybrida *'Nonstop Hybrid Mixed'*
Left: Antirrhinum majus *'Burpee's Double Supreme Hybrid Mixed'*

T; most are Native American from Central and South America; challenging to grow from seed, easy from started plants.
❀ ◐ ●
Height: 6 to 12 inches.
Colors: White, pink, rose, red tones.
Characteristics: There is a great diversity in the foliage and flowers of the thousands of varieties of begonias. The two most popular varieties for American gardens are the wax begonia and the tuberous begonia. Green to bronze leaves, with clusters of free-flowering single or double flowers characterize the wax begonia. The tuberous begonias have large single or double

Begonia semperflorens
'Vodka', 'Whisky', and
'Gin'

flowers that may resemble those of the camellias. Very adaptable plants, remaining in flower all summer and performing in all kinds of weather with good foliage and neat appearance. They are valued as a showy plant for shady locations as well as a long-blooming pot plant. The wax begonia's green-leaved varieties usually perform better in full sun than the bronze-leaved varieties.

The begonia 'Wings', a Burpee breeding breakthrough, blooms in three months or less from seed with the biggest wax begonia flowers we've seen—up to 3 inches across. The plants are bushy and base-branching, growing 10 to 12 inches and holding their flowers well above the foliage to show them off. 'Cocktail Mix' is another good variety for edging. All are good winter houseplants or cool greenhouse plants.

Tuberous begonias come in a wide variety of color and form.

They can be single-flowered, ruffled, full-double, or camellia-form with flowers measuring from 5 to 6½ inches across. The colors can be single or accented with a contrasting edge. There are upright growing, compact or full branched, pendulous varieties, ideal for bedding, container, or hanging basket.

The Pacific Giant ruffled series and the Hanging Giant Double Hybrids were developed by three generations of leading California begonia breeders and are especially suited to American gardens. The Nonstop Hybrids are an outstanding series of compact plants with double and semidouble flowers that exhibit excellent heat tolerance. They are ideal for southern gardens. *Cultural Information:* Both kinds of begonias are available from seed. If starting from seed, be careful as you open the packet. Begonia seeds are very small (if you don't look closely, you might think there are no seeds in the packet at all). Make sure your planting medium is moist and ready when you open the seed pack. Sow seeds on top of the plant medium and cover with a glass pane or clear plastic to keep the medium from drying out until the plants appear. They need light and heat to germinate. Growing under lights and keeping a bottom heat of 70 degrees Fahrenheit help speed germination. Seedlings have extremely fine root systems and a weak solution of liquid fertilizer weekly in the early days, before transplanting, will help prevent them from starving as they quickly deplete the nutrients in the planting medium. Once established, the plants

don't require weekly feeding. Growing wax begonia from seed is best tried by the gardener with indoor growing experience. Propagation from cuttings is easier.

'Christmas' and 'Rex' begonias can easily be propagated from leaves. Cut through several veins on the underside of a leaf and pin the leaf onto a moist planting medium. (I use hairpins to be sure the veins are touching the soil.) Put the container in a plastic bag to keep it moist until plants begin to sprout at the places where the vein was cut. Three or four plants can be produced from one leaf. Once plants are established, move them to individual pots.

Houseplants should be kept in an cool area with a lot of light but only a few hours of direct sunlight. Plants need repotting only when the roots fill the pot.

The tuberous varieties do best in climates with cool, damp nights. Protection from wind and afternoon sun is essential. Soil should be rich—well-drained but moisture-retentive. For blooms from early summer 'til frost, start the bulbs indoors in March. Fill flats or pots with peat moss and press the bulbs into the surface, curved side down. Set them in a bright spot, 72 to 80 degrees Fahrenheit, and keep them evenly damp. Reduce temperature to 65 degrees when growth begins. When they are about 4 inches tall, transfer the plants to the garden or into the containers where they are to bloom. Space them 8 to 10 inches apart. In fall, when the leaves turn yellow and begin to drop, lift the bulbs, remove the stems, and store the bulbs in a cool, dry place until it is time to replant them in the spring.

The wax begonias are one of the few flowers that bloom under almost any light conditions, but they do best in light shade. They bloom continuously all summer and are rarely damaged by wind, rain, or pests. Space 6 to 8 inches apart.

Days to germinate: 14 to 21; Germination temperature: 70 to 80 degrees Fahrenheit; Growth temperature: 60 to 70 degrees Fahrenheit: Days to bloom: 85 to 130; Weeks to start indoors: 8 to 12 before last frost for wax begonias and 4 to 6 months for tuberous begonias.

Uses: Edging, bedding, houseplant, rock garden, container.

Bells of Ireland; see *Moluccella*

Black-eyed Susan vine; see *Thunbergia*

Blanket flower; see *Gaillardia*

Blue daisy; see *Felicia*

Blue lace flower; see *Trachymene*

Brachycome (bra-kee-KŌ-mee) **swan river daisy,** HH, moderate. ○
Height: 9 to 15 inches.
Colors: Rose, blue, violet, white.
Characteristics: Swan river daisy is a compact bushy grower imported from Australia that performs well in containers and hanging baskets. Fragrant with light green, fine, lacy foliage and sweet-scented daisy flow-

ers. The flowers can be cut for small bouquets.

Cultural Information: Prefer a rich soil but do well in ordinary garden soil. Appreciate moderate feeding of 5–10–5 through the season. Brachycome bloom for six weeks or more if dead flowers are removed. For flowers all season, make successive plantings at three-week intervals. Space 6 to 8 inches apart.

Days to germinate: 14; Germination temperature; 60 to 65 degrees Fahrenheit; Growth temperature: 70 to 75 degrees Fahrenheit; Days to bloom: 70; Weeks to start indoors: 4 to 6.

Uses: Border, container, hanging basket, edging.

Browallia (brō-AH-lee-a) HH, Native American from Colombia, easy. ◑ ○
Height: 9 to 10 inches.
Colors: Shades of blue, white, and lavender.
Characteristics: Star-shaped flowers cover these vigorous plants whose branching habit makes them particularly fine for hanging baskets. Grows well in shady locations. The genus is best known for its steel blue varieties.

'Blue Bells Improved' has violet-blue flowers (1 to 2 inches across) that turn lavender-blue and require no pinching to stay bushy. 'Jingle Bells' comes in shades of blue, white and lavender.

Cultural Information: The seeds need light to germinate; do not cover with soil. During summer, pinch back to maintain neat shape and encourage flowering. If growing a browallia in a container, keep its roots snug,

Top: Mixed colors, Brachycome
Above: Browallia 'Blue Bells Improved'

or potbound, and be careful not to overfeed or overwater or you will have leaves and no flowers. Browallias like high humidity and suffer in hot, dry air. A daily misting is highly beneficial.

This plant often self-sows in protected beds or warmer climates. Space 6 to 8 inches apart.

Days to germinate: 15 to 21; Germination temperature: 70 to 80 degrees Fahrenheit; Growth temperature: 60 to 70 degrees Fahrenheit; Days to bloom: 95 to 110; Weeks before last frost to start indoors 8 to 10.

Uses: Hanging basket, container, border.

Top: Callistephus chinensis *'Burpee's Dwarf Border Mixed'*
Above: Calendula officinalis *'Dwarf Gem Mixed'*

Butterfly flower; see *Schizanthus*

Busy lizzy; see *Impatiens*

Calendula (ka-LEN-dew-la) **pot marigold,** H, easy. ✳ ▮ ✾ ○ ◑
Height: 12 inches for dwarf varieties, 18 to 25 inches for tall varieties.
Colors: Orange, yellow, gold.
Characteristics: Bushy plants with large flowers, usually one to a stem. The many-petalled flowers are up to 4 inches across, in bright, sunny colors. In arrangements, they are long-lasting. The long, narrow leaves are slightly sticky to the touch. Calendula flowers are occasionally used as a substitute for saffron, to add deep yellow color to cheeses, sauces, and soups.

They can also be added to tea for flavor and color. Sprinkled on salads, the petals add flavor and color. If the flowers are picked in bud for bouquets, they will open and keep longer.
Cultural Information: These plants prefer cool weather and average well-drained soil. They thrive in northern climates with cool summers. Sow seeds outdoors in early spring in the North, fall and winter in the South and Pacific Coast areas, where winters are mild. They will do well in a cool greenhouse in the winter. As a greenhouse or indoor plant, it is almost ever-blooming when it enjoys cool nights of 55 degrees Fahrenheit. Pick off dead flower heads to encourage more bloom. Seeds are large and pot marigold, so easy to grow, makes an excellent child's garden plant. Reseeds readily, but often reverts to smaller, single types, so it may be preferable to purchase new plants or seeds yearly.

In Zones 8 through 10 (see the USDA Plant Hardiness Map, page 94), pot marigolds can be planted in early fall for long winter and spring bloom. In northern climates it can be started indoors as it transplants easily into the garden. Space dwarf varieties 8 inches, tall varieties 12 inches.
Days to germinate: 10 to 15; Germination temperature: 70 degrees Fahrenheit; Growth temperature: 70 degrees Fahrenheit; Days to bloom: 58 to 90; Weeks to start indoors: 6 to 8.
Uses: Border, cutting, greenhouse plant, child's garden.

California poppy; see *Eschscholzia*

Callistephus (ka-LEE-ste-fus) **garden aster, China aster,** HH, easy. ▮ ○
Height: 6 to 9 inches for dwarf varieties, 2 to 3 feet for tall varieties.
Colors: White, pinks, rose, scarlet, lavender, purple.
Characteristics: Asters come in many flower styles, from daisy-like single to fluffy double, mum- and peony-flowered, with straight to curled petals. They make wonderful cut flowers, but are an exception to the rule "the more you cut the more they bloom." Once cut, the plants do not continue to bloom. Each plant will have blooms for four to six weeks. Different varieties of asters bloom at different times—early, mid-season, and late—so you can plan your planting for longer seasonal bloom. If you supplement daylight with fluorescent light, you can grow asters as flowering houseplants, in winter. (Not many plants will bloom in winter with daylight only.)

'Pot'n Patio' dwarf asters do bloom indoors during the short days of winter and early spring without additional light. 'Totem Pole' asters are a living bouquet, as each plant has eight to ten, long (2-foot), strong, upright stems topped by giant, fully double flowers 4½ to 5 inches across. Since the flowers will not rebloom, you can pull up the whole plant, cut off the roots and put it in water, and use it as a bouquet.

Burpee's Ribbon series, in pink and blue, is an excellent choice for the long, hot summers in southern zones.
Cultural Information: Prefers limey, fertile, well-drained soil.

Don't grow in the same location two years in a row as they are susceptible to fungus diseases that build up in the soil. Asters don't like to be transplanted so it's best to start them in peat pots. When sowing outdoors, protect the tiny seed with a garden blanket to prevent it from washing away in heavy spring rains.

Asters are very shallow-rooted and the use of mulch will help keep soil and roots cool and moist. Don't let them dry out during periods of drought. Depending on size, space between 8 and 10 inches apart.

Days to germinate: 10 to 14; Germination temperature: 65 to 70 degrees Fahrenheit; Growth temperature: 60 to 70 degrees Fahrenheit; Days to bloom: 70 to 90; Start indoors 4 to 6 weeks.

Uses: Cutting, border.

Candytuft; see *Iberis*

Cape daisy; see *Venidium*

Cape marigold; see *Dimorphotheca*

Catharanthus roseus

(ka-tha-RAN-thus ro-see-us) **periwinkle, vinca,** T, Native American, moderate. ◊ ☀ ❀ ○ ◑
Height: 4 to 18 inches.
Colors: White, rose, pink; some with red eye or center.
Characteristics: These plants have been called "impatiens of the sun" and they do resemble the bushy habit and flat, round flowers of impatiens. Like impatiens, periwinkles are really short-lived perennials. Their flowers are set off by their dark green, glossy leaves. They can

provide continuous bloom through even the hot, dry summers of the Southwest, and thrive in cities as air pollution doesn't bother them. A greeting of vinca, lining a sunny walk to the front door, will look good all summer and well into the fall.

The Carpet series is excellent for hanging baskets or flowering carpets, reaching 6 inches high and spreading 24 inches.

Periwinkles are low perennial shrubs in tropical America. They do not make good cut flowers. Don't confuse *Catharanthus* with Vinca minor, a popular, glossy, evergreen, perennial groundcover. Their flower shapes are similar but they behave differently.

Cultural Information: Periwinkles prefer to be kept evenly moist in average, well-drained soils, but will tolerate heat and drought. It is best to start them indoors because cool temperatures reduce germination. Don't plant them out until night temperatures stay above 50 degrees Fahrenheit. Periwinkles do not like cool soils, and overwatering will cause the seedlings to yellow and die. Seedlings are slow starters but the established plants are great performers, blooming continuously until frost. They will self-sow in warm areas and are rarely bothered by insects or disease. Upright varieties are spaced 12 inches apart.

Days to germinate: 10 to 14; Germination temperature: 70 to 75 degrees Fahrenheit; Growth temperature: 65 to 70 degrees Fahrenheit; Days to bloom: 80 to 90; Weeks to start indoors: 12.

Uses: Groundcover, edging, container.

Celosia (se-LO-see-a) cockscomb HH, easy. ◊ ☀ ❙ ❀ ○ ◑

Height: 6 inches to 3 feet.
Colors: Red, yellow, pink, orange.
Characteristics: An old-fashioned favorite for cutting and drying. With crested flowers, *C. cristata* resembles a rooster's comb, blooms midsummer to frost, and needs little care. The plumed varieties, *C. plumosa*, are showy, well-branched plants crowned with silky, feathery plumes, from midsummer to frost. The dried plumes make long-lasting bouquets and the bright colors are perfect for holiday decorations. I use them to decorate evergreen wreaths.

'New Look', AAS-winner, has dwarf plants with intense scarlet plumes and deep bronze foliage, attractive even before it blooms. The color holds well; plants resist damage from heat,

Top: Catharanthus roseus *'Magic Carpet'*
Above: Celosia *'New Look'*

Top: Centaurea cyanus *'Blue Boy'*
Above: Cineraria maritima *'Silver Dust'*

rain, and wind. 'Fancy Plumes', 'Century', 'Floradale', and 'Castle' are all good varieties and 'Jewel Box Red' is an exceptional cultivar specially suited to Southern gardens.

Cultural Information: Average soil is required. Celosias are heat-loving plants that tolerate drought. These plants are sensitive to both cold temperatures and root disturbances, and if you're not careful, they might respond by not blooming. Take three precautions: Water seedlings with lukewarm water; start indoors in individual cells or pots (not flats) that won't disturb roots when transplanting; harden off slowly, only moving to the garden when night temperatures stay about 60 degrees Fahrenheit. If their growth is interrupted by cold temperatures or by becoming potbound, they produce small flowers early and are unlikely to grow to full size or full flower.

If using as a dry flower, cut before the flower begins to go to seed. Strip the leaves, wire the stem to give support and treat as you would other dry flowers (see page 93). Depending on size, space them from 8 inches to 2 feet.

Days to germinate: 8 to 14; Germination temperature: 70 degrees Fahrenheit; Growth temperature: 65 to 70 degrees Fahrenheit; Days to bloom: 75 to 100; Weeks to start 4 to 6.

Uses: Bedding, container, cutting, and drying.

Centaurea cyanus (sent-OW-ree-a see-AH-nus) **bachelor's button, cornflower, *Centaurea imperialis*** (sent-OW-ree-a im-per-ee-AL-is) **sweet sultan, H, easy.** ◖ ◗ ○

Height: C. cyanus: 12 to 30 inches, *C. imperialis:* 3 feet.

Colors: C. cyanus: White, carmine, pink, lavender, *C. imperialis:* Blue, pink, red, white.

Characteristics: C. cyanus, bachelor's buttons, are thought by many to be native American wildflowers. However, *C. cyanus* is the national flower of Germany and was brought to America in the seventeenth century. It has since escaped from the garden to beautify our roadsides. This is an old-fashioned flower, popular for good reason. The best-known are the small, round, ruffled, blue flowers—an ideal buttonhole flower, as they last several days without water. As a cut flower in water, it can last two weeks or longer. Breeders have expanded the range of colors and developed plants that are better behaved, with more compact habits, in the garden. The double flowers are very showy. Tall types are good for the back of the border; dwarf types have a neat, bushlike habit. Grow 'Blue Boy' for blue flowers, 'Pinkie' for pink flowers and 'Snowman' for white flowers.

C. imperialis has very large, fringed, furry-looking sweet-scented flowers in delicate tints ranging from white, pink, and carmine to lavender. Massing helps the delicate flowers to appear showy in the garden. They bloom a long time and are long-lasting cut flowers. Toothed leaves—the foliage is medium green—make this a very bushy, upright plant.

Cultural Information: Sow in early spring right where you want them. Bachelor's buttons are exceptionally adaptable and grow rapidly in poor, sandy, or average soils. Fertilizer is not necessary unless the soil is unusually poor. They prefer cool weather but take heat and drought well. They need regular deadheading of spent blooms or reseeding to extend the flower period. The taller plants are inclined to sprawl and may need staking. Space plants 8 to 10 inches apart.

C. cyanus: Days to germinate: 10

to 21; Germination temperature: 60 to 65 degrees Fahrenheit; Growth temperature: 60 to 65 degrees Fahrenheit; Days to bloom 60 to 70.

C. imperialis: Days to germinate: 10 to 15; Germination temperature: 70 to 75 degrees Fahrenheit; Growth temperature: 65 to 70 degrees Fahrenheit; Days to bloom: 60 to 80.

Uses: Drying, cutting, border.

China aster; see **Calliste-phus**

Cineraria maritima (sin-ne-RAH-ee-a ma-ri-TEE-ma) **Dusty Miller, Silverdust,** HH, easy. ◉ ❋ ○

Height: 12 inches.

Colors: Silver foliage.

Characteristics: Finely cut, silvery white, velvety foliage that will add interest to the flower garden, and complement and enhance the color of surrounding flowers, especially those of the blue family. It makes a wonderful edging for a garden and can effectively be alternated with ageratums, or planted in front of *Salvia farinacea,* as they complement each other.

Dusty Miller is really a quick-growing foliage perennial with yellow button flowers its second year in southern zones. In northern gardens it is best grown as an annual. *C. maritima* is easily confused with *Chrysanthemum ptarmiciflorum,* Dusty Miller, Silver Lace, which grows to 24 inches but is in all other respects very similar to Dusty Miller, Silverdust.

Cultural Information: These plants like ordinary, well-drained or poor, sandy soil. It takes heat and drought well, but appreciates a good watering during prolonged hot, dry weather. Silverdust is grown for its beautiful foliage. There is confusion over the proper Latin name; it was formerly known as *Senecio cineraria.* Space plants 6 inches apart.

Days to germinate: 10 to 15; Germination temperature: 70 to 75 degrees Fahrenheit; Growth temperature: 60 to 65 degrees Fahrenheit; Days to decorative rosette: 60; Days to maturity: 90.

Uses: Edging, accent border, cutting, container, rock garden.

Clarkia amoena (KLARK-ee-a a-MOY-na) **farewell-to-spring,** H, Native American, moderately easy. ❋ ◉ ❀ ○ ◑

Height: 1 to 3 feet.

Colors: White, pink, salmon, lavender, bicolors.

Characteristics: An American native wildflower from the Rocky Mountains, where it roams freely. It is named after Captain William Clark, who collected seed on the Lewis and Clark expedition. The wild form has single pink blooms, but breeders have tamed it, introducing larger clusters of 1- to 2-inch cup-shaped, single or double, plain or ruffled flowers on slender wiry stems. A very free-flowering plant (it doesn't require deadheading or other help to keep it in flower), blooming from midsummer to fall. It is also a good, long-lasting cut flower. Sometimes the Latin name is listed as *Godetia.*

Clarkia amoena *'Grace Hybrid Rose'* and *'Grace Hybrid Pink'*

Cultural Information: This plant is not too fussy and thrives in ordinary soil. Sow in spring, as soon as the ground can be worked, for bloom from midsummer into fall. It grows faster in cool weather and can be planted so early outside that there is no reason to start indoors. It is best to sow where plants are to grow. It does not tolerate heat well and will slow-bloom in hot summers, reviving when the weather cools. It sets seeds easily but if you remove the faded flowers you can further prolong the long-flowering season. Pinch back for more compact plants.

In Zones 8 through 10 (see the USDA Plant Hardiness Map, page 94), seeds can be sown outdoors in the fall for early spring bloom. Space 8 to 10 inches apart.

Days to germinate: 7 to 14; Germination temperature: 60 degrees Fahrenheit; Growth temperature: 60 degrees Fahrenheit; Days to bloom: 65 to 80; Does well direct sown.

Uses: Border, cutting.

Cleome (klee-O-mee) **spider plant,** H, tropical Native American, easy. ◐ ✻ ❚ ❀ ○ ◑
Height: 3 to 5 feet.
Colors: White, pinks, purple, burgundy.
Characteristics: Tall, rapid-growing, weather-resistant plants, spider plants have seed pods that develop and dangle, like spider legs, under the big airy flower clusters. The flowers are haloed by an outer circle of long, graceful stamens. On bright sunny days, the flower petals will curl up and open again as evening approaches. Even curled, the flowers are showy. This free-flowering plant makes wonderful long-lasting cut flowers, and when kept out of direct sun, the petals stay open all the time.

When grown in a row, the plants create a temporary hedge 3 feet wide and are useful to screen out an unsightly area. If planted at the back of a small garden, four plants are enough to cover an area 9 feet by 3 feet. Plants can be leafless and leggy at the bottom so it is best to plant in front of them.

When cutting for bouquets, be careful to hold the flower on the main stem between branches. A thorn is located at every place where a flowering branch joins the stem. The leaves and stems are sticky to the touch. Flowers have a pungent, lemony fragrance.

'Pink Queen', 'Purple Queen', 'Snow Queen', and 'Helen Campbell' are all popular varieties that produce large, airy, delicate flowers. *Cleome lutea* or the yellow bee plant is a native American annual from California and Colorado.

Cultural Information: This plant tolerates heat and drought and performs well direct sown outside after all danger of frost. It sets seeds easily. The seed pods form directly under the flower while the flower is still blooming and add interest; they need not be removed. You can remove faded flowers to help the plant branch and produce more flowers. However, cleomes are long-flowering even while prolifically producing seed. Whether you cut off spent flowers or not, the plants will bloom until killed by hard prolonged frost. Each individual flower lasts for several weeks. These plants frequently reseed, but the seedlings may revert in color and be weedy-looking. Can be grown next to a fence to which stems can be tied if support is needed. Cleomes should be spaced 2 feet apart. They are not easily bothered by pests or disease.
Days to germinate: 12 to 21; Germination temperature: 70 to 80 degrees Fahrenheit; Growth temperature: 60 to 65 degrees Fahrenheit; Days to bloom: 60 to 70; Weeks to start indoors: 4 to 6.
Uses: Back of the border, cutting, temporary hedge, or shrub.

Clockvine; see Annual Vines: ***Thunbergia***

Cockscomb; see ***Celosia***

Coleus (KO-lee-us) **foliage plant,** T, moderately easy. ◑ ○ ●
Height: 12 to 21 inches.
Colors: Whites, greens, pink, reds, scarlets, browns, oranges, combined in multicolor or bicolor foliage.

Characteristics: Bold, bright, multicolor and bicolor foliage combinations that would shock, if combined by anyone but Mother Nature. Coleuses are really quick-growing, tender perennial herbs from Java. They belong to the same family of plants as mints.

Coleuses are grown for their rainbow-colored foliage, which turns shady areas into kaleidoscopes of color. They are excellent for striking accents, as a background for low-growing annuals or for an oriental carpet groundcover. Use them to beautify the north or east side of your house, under trees or shrubs, or on shady patios or porches.

There are several different varieties of coleus based on their different leaf sizes and shapes: small and tapered or small-lobed to large fringed, heart-shaped and lobed. The richly colored leaves are often deeply cut or toothed around the edges.

Coleuses thrive in pots, baskets, and other containers. In the winter, they can be grown indoors or they can be brought in from the garden and grown as houseplants.

The whorls of small blue and lavender flowers held in spikes are insignificant and should be removed to prevent the plant from going to seed and to encourage the growth of more foliage. The flowers at the bottom of the spike sprout into seed pods first, dangling like spider legs from the stem.

The Wizard series features 10-inch plants with large, heart-shaped leaves that have a bushy habit and don't need pinching back. The Carefree series has small, deeply lobed leaves, available in a variety of colors.
Cultural Information: This plant needs light during germination. Keep seedlings and plants moist during the growing season. The young seedlings will be green, developing their colorful foliage as they mature. Mulch will help both garden and pot plants stay moist.

Cuttings made in late summer are so easy to grow they can be rooted in water and potted up for indoor plants and gifts for friends. Seeds can be sown any time for indoor houseplants. Pinch back new growth to induce bushiness. They grow well in any good, well-drained soil. The colors are more vivid when grown in partial shade. Space plants 8 to 10 inches apart. Days to germinate: 10 to 15; Germination temperature: 65 to 75 degrees Fahrenheit; Growth temperature: 60 to 70 degrees Fahrenheit; Days to bloom 60 to 75; Weeks to start indoors: 6 to 8.
Uses: Groundcover, accent, shady border, container and window box, houseplant.

Consolida orientalis

(kon-SO-li-da) **larkspur** H, somewhat challenging. ✳ ❚ ○ ◖
Height: 2 to 4 feet.
Colors: White, pink, light blue, dark blue.
Characteristics: Elegant, stately stalks with single or double florets and fine, light green foliage provide splendid masses of color in a border or growing wild on a sunny slope (which is where I sow them each fall as part of a meadow mix. I find them easier to grow this way as I'm not depending on them to

fill a spot in the border, and I always have plenty to pick for fresh or dried bouquets.) Consolidas are outstanding as long-lasting cut flowers and easy to dry, retaining their bright colors all winter long.

Burpee's 'Giant Imperial' is tall and graceful, with densely flowering spikes.

Don't confuse larkspur with the delphinium, which has a thicker flower stalk, tighter clusters of large flowers, and bulbous roots. You will sometimes find larkspur mistakenly listed under *Delphinium ajacis.*
Cultural Information: Seeds should be direct sown in fall or early spring. Seed planted outdoors in the fall, even in northern zones, will bloom in early spring. In northern climates, sow late enough so the seed will not germinate before heavy freezing. The advantage is that the seed will germinate very early in the spring and flower earlier than seed not planted until spring. In southern areas, plant six to seven weeks before frost to give the plants time to become established. The plants

Consolida orientalis
'Giant Imperial Mixed'

Opposite, from top:
Cleome 'Queen Mixed';
Coleus blumei
'Wizard Mixed'; Coleus blumei 'Wizard
Rose' (left); Coleus blumei 'Wizard Red'
(right); and Coleus blumei 'Wizard
Sunset'.

Cosmos 'Sensation'

will winter over in all but exceptionally hard winters.

Keep well watered but not soggy. Cultivate and mulch to control weeds. It prefers a cool growing season and doesn't like transplanting. All parts of the plant are poisonous. Space 6 to 8 inches apart. Days to germinate: 20 to 28; Germination temperature: 65 to 70 degrees Fahrenheit; Days to bloom: 75; Weeks before last frost to start indoors: 6 to 8.
Uses: Cutting, border, drying.

Cornflower; *Centaurea*

Corn poppy; see *Papaver*

Cosmos (KOS-mos) HH, Native American from Mexico, easy. ◗ ❋ ❚ ❀ ○
Height: 2½ to 4 feet.
Colors: Cosmos sulphureus: yellow, orange, red; *Cosmos bipin-*

natus: pinks, purple, burgundy, white.
Characteristics: Graceful summer-flowering plants that attract butterflies. *Cosmos bipinnatus* has finely divided, feathery foliage with single daisylike 3- to 5-inch flowers and wide serrated petals in white, pinks, burgundy, and rose-crimson. Cosmos are such prolific bloomers that cutting flowers from them frequently improves the garden's display. My favorites for long-lasting bouquets are: 'Sensation', pink, white, and purple with open flowers, 'Seashell', same colors but with curved petals forming a pinwheel; and 'Candystripe', with petals outlined in red. *Cosmos sulphureus* has double round 2- to 2½-inch yellow, orange or red flowers. Foliage resembles marigold foliage. The best variety is 'Bright Lights'. They are smaller plants (3 feet) in colors of yellow, orange, and red.
Cultural Information: Cosmos performs in any soil, even poor or sandy, as long as it has good drainage. It takes both heat and drought. Water sparingly to avoid root or stem rot in soggy soils. Cosmos seems to thrive on neglect and will reseed but not necessarily where you want it. It can grow nicely against a fence, but usually doesn't need support unless grown in a windy spot. So easy to direct sow (after all danger of frost), you won't gain much by starting indoors; if you do, they will transplant easily. Prefers light for germination. It is better not to fertilize these plants, as too much nitrogen will bring foliage without flowers until late in the sea-

son. Space taller varieties 2 feet apart and shorter varieties 1 foot apart. Some taller varieties need staking.
Days to germinate: 14; Germination temperature: 65 to 70 degrees Fahrenheit; Growth temperature: 65 degrees Fahrenheit; Days to bloom: 65; Weeks before last frost to start indoors: 6 to 8.
Uses: Cutting, back of border.

Cupflower; see *Nierembergia*

Dahlberg daisy; see *Dysodia*

Dahlia (DAH-lee-a) HH, Native American, moderate. ❚ ❀ ○ ◐
Height: 1 to 5 feet.
Colors: All colors except blue.
Characteristics: Flowers are round and varied: single, double, cactus, pompon, peony, quilled. Foliage comes in medium to dark green and deep burgundy. Dahlias are not ordinarily grown for their foliage, but varieties with burgundy leaves give the gardener a double pleasure: striking, contrasting foliage and large flowers. There are dwarf varieties with large 2- to 3-inch flowers for the front of the border, medium for the middle and tall varieties for the back of the border that can also be grown as a floral hedge. Some continue blooming late in the fall, after light frost and right up to heavy frost. The most difficult thing about them is deciding which variety to grow. Dahlias are originally from Mexico but have been extensively bred for larger, showier flowers that no longer resemble their ancestors.

Dahlias are long-lasting cut flowers for bouquets or for floating singly in a bowl or birdbath. *Cultural Information:* The taller varieties will need to be staked. They love a soil full of organic matter. If you grow them for entry in a county fair or would prefer fewer but more spectacular flowers, disbud lateral buds (the buds along the stem, rather than terminal buds, those at the tip) to encourage exhibition-sized flowers. If using as cut flowers, the end of each stem must be sealed by dipping in boiling water.

After leaves are blackened by frost, dig up the tubers that have formed over the summer and store in dry peat moss for next year's even-bushier plants with even-larger flowers. Space dwarf plants 12 inches apart and tall varieties 3 feet apart.

Days to germinate: 10 to 20; Germination temperature: 70 to 75 degrees Fahrenheit; Growth temperature: 60 to 65 degrees Fahrenheit; Days to bloom: 70; Weeks to start indoors: 8.
Uses: Cutting, container, border, temporary hedge.

Daisy, African; see *Dimorphotheca*

Daisy, blue; see *Felicia*

Daisy, Cape; see *Venidium*

Daisy, Dahlberg; see *Dyssodia*

Daisy, swan river; see *Brachycome*

Daisy, Transvaal; see *Gerbera*

Delphinium ajacis*; see *Consolida

Above:
Clockwise, from top left:
Medium height Dahlia *'Pari Tahi Sunrise';*
Colorette Dahlia *'Dandy'; Dwarf* Dahlia *'Pink Princess'; Dwarf border* Dahlia *'Bonnie Esperance' (close-up).*

Top: Pompom Dahlia *'Potgieter'*
Center: Dwarf border Dahlia *'Bonnie Esperance'*
Bottom: Peony Dahlia *'Japanese Bishop'*

Top: Dianthus
'Telstar Picotee Hybrid'
Above: Dimorphotheca
aurantiaca

Dianthus (dee-ANTH-us) **pinks, sweet William, carnation,** H, moderately easy. ✳ 🌡 ❀ ○
Height: 6 to 12 inches.
Colors: White, salmon, pink, scarlet, crimson, purple, bicolors.
Characteristics: An old-fashioned garden favorite with single or double, fringed or plain blooms. Some varieties have a sweet-spicy scent, although not as fragrant as the perennial varieties. Cultivation and breeding have added to the number of its petals and to variations in color. There are hundreds of species of *Dianthus* but the four that follow are the most popular for the annual garden.

D. chinensis has beautiful flowers that paint themselves in an infinity of shades, from light rose to pure white, from deep red to the hue of a glowing fire. The same flower puts on contrasting, yet blending, tints. Pure white is pricked with crimson, and the rose color is streaked with a vivid and brilliant red. *D. chinensis* may be marbled or spotted with areas of contrasting color. The pink is nearly as varied in form as in color. It is flat, double-shaped like a rose, and always retains its delicate fragrance. The foliage colors range from light green to blue-green with long narrow leaves and it frequently will reseed itself, reappearing year after year.

Originally Asiatic, short-lived perennials, they have been hybridized for earlier bloom and wider color range.

D. bicolor was the University of Georgia's 1986 gold medal winner for superb southern garden performance.

'Magic Charms', 'Telstars' and 'Princess' are all dependable varieties.

D. barbatus (sweet William) is a biennial, normally flowering the second summer from seed. However, where growing seasons are long or when started indoors ten weeks before last frost, this species will bloom in late summer.

D. caryophyllus (carnation) is one of the best long-lasting cut flowers. Similar to the carnations available from florists, they are smaller flowered and more fragrant, adding a spicy perfume to a whole room. In mild areas, it is perennial or biennial. In northern climates, grow as an annual.

Cultural Information: All of these species resent wet soils and are susceptible to rotting at the soil line. They prefer sandy, alkaline, well-drained soil and cool, rather than hot, summers. Fertilize with superphosphate, available at garden centers, to encourage strong roots. It is important to remove dead flowers to encourage new blooms and prevent plants from going to seed.

New plants can be propagated from cuttings and held over in a cold frame in Zones 3 through 7 (see The USDA Plant Hardiness Map, page 94). Space 6 inches apart.

Days to germinate: 7 to 14; Germination temperature: 65 to 70 degrees Fahrenheit; Growth for temperature: 65 degrees Fahrenheit; Days to bloom: 65 to 110.

Uses: Cutting, edging, border, container.

Dimorphotheca auran- tiaca (dy-mor-fo-THEE-ka or-AN- tee-ah-ka) **African daisy, Cape marigold,** T, moderate.
💧 ✴ 🌡 ○
Height: 1 foot.
Colors: Yellow, salmon, apricot, white, all with dark eye.
Characteristics: An excellent choice for hot, dry areas. The large daisy flowers, 3½ to 4 inches across, bloom profusely for a six-week period. To extend the bloom, make succession plantings and flowers will bloom right up to frost. The flowers close at night, flaunting

easily propagated by division of one- or two-year-old clumps. (Each division should have two or more growing points.) When growing gerberas from seed, a mix of 60 percent perlite/40 percent peat is best because gerberas likes a slightly acid, well-drained soil and a moist atmosphere. Using bottom heat to maintain a soil temperature of 68 degrees Fahrenheit, avoiding direct sunlight and keeping the soil mix evenly moist will give good germination results.

Always use fresh seed; it doesn't have a long shelf life. When planting, place the sharp end of the seed pointed down and make sure the other end gets light to help it germinate. When transplanting, the crowns should not be buried. Space 12 to 15 inches apart.

Days to germinate: 10 to 18; Germination temperature: 70 to 75 degrees Fahrenheit; Growth temperature: 60 to 65 degrees Fahrenheit; Days to bloom: 125 to 140; Weeks to start indoors: 8 to 10.

Uses: Border, container, cutting.

Globe amaranth; see *Gom-phrena*

Godetia; see *Clarkia*

Golden fleece; see *Dys-sodia*

Gomphrena globosa
(gom-FREE-na glo-BO-sa) **globe amaranth, HH, easy.** ● ✳
🌡 ❀ ○
Height: 1½ to 2 feet.
Colors: White, pink, red, purple, orange.
Characteristics: An everlasting, with cloverlike strawflowers in shimmering, iridescent colors.

The plants grow upright and bushy with dark green foliage. Some varieties have red stems.

'Buddy', a dwarf variety, grows to 9 inches, with flowers 1½ inches across that virtually cover the plants; it is available in many colors.

Cultural Information: This plant tolerates drought and heat, but needs water to endure extended periods. To speed germination, soak in lukewarm water three or four days and then spread the wet, cottony seed mass over the top of the soil in a thin layer. If starting indoors, transplant out into the garden when the trees start to leaf out. Space dwarf varieties 6 to 8 inches apart, large varieties 12 inches. Days to germinate: 14 to 20; Germination temperature: 70 to 75 degrees Fahrenheit; Growth temperature: 65 to 70 degrees Fahrenheit; Days to flower: 70 to 80; Weeks before last frost to start indoors: 6 to 8.

Uses: Drying, border, cutting.

Gypsophila elegans (jip-SOF-i-la ay-le-ganz) **baby's breath, H, easy.** 🌡 ○
Height: 15 to 18 inches.
Colors: White, rose.
Characteristics: Each flower is a perfect miniature formed by five tiny petals. They bloom in mass with many small, dainty flowers (¼ inch across) on slender stems, creating a frothy, airy appearance above lance-shaped leaves. This plant is a wonderful cut flower, very quick to bloom but short-lived (5 to 6 weeks). It is easier to grow it in a cut flower garden than a border, which will need reseeding every two to three weeks for summer-long bloom.

Top: Mixed colors Gomphrena globosa
Above: Gypsophila elegans 'Covent Garden White'

'Covent Garden White' has masses of pure white flowers on many branched, long stems. The rose-colored varieties are temperamental and not recommended.

Cultural Information: This plant thrives in any well-drained, non-acid (add lime) garden soil. It is best to sow seed where it is to grow; pat seeds gently into place, as they sprout faster when in firm contact with the soil. After plants are established, allow the soil to dry out between watering. Plants need proper spacing or they become leggy

Top: Helichrysum bracteatum
Above left: Heliotropium arborescens *'Dwarf Marine'*
Above right: Helianthus annua *'Jumbo'*

and floppy. Sometimes plants reseed and rebloom themselves in the same season but this is not a dependable occurrence. Space 8 inches apart.
Days to germinate: 10 to 14; Germination temperature: 65 to 70 degrees Fahrenheit; Growth temperature: 60 to 70 degrees Fahrenheit; Days to bloom: about 45; Weeks to start indoors: 6 to 8.
Uses: Cutting.

Helianthus annuus (hee-lee-ANTH-us AN-ew-us) **sunflower,** H, Native American from Minnesota to California, easy. ☀ 🌡 ○ ◑

Height: 2 to 12 feet.
Colors: Yellow, gold, mahogany-red, brown.
Characteristics: Standing at attention, a regiment of sunflowers makes a decorative screen.

Large, dahlialike single or double flowers that grow rapidly to tower above everything else in the garden make them a favorite with children. The plant has coarse, rough, hairy leaves. Some varieties, 'Mammoth' and 'D 131', for example, are grown for their edible seeds—delicious roasted or made into sunflower butter (same principal as peanut butter). Varieties like 'Color Fashion' (height 5 feet) and 'Teddy Bear' (height 2 feet) are grown for their ornamental value rather than for seed.
Cultural Information: Sunflowers grow rapidly, so there is no need to start seeds indoors. Direct seed after all danger of frost is past. They prefer light, dry, well-drained soil and tolerate heat. Water only during prolonged drought. Little or no fertilizer is needed unless the soil is very poor. For larger varieties, plant two or three seeds together, then thin seedlings to one every 2 to 4 feet. Dwarf varieties can be 1 foot or closer.
Days to germinate: 14 to 21; Germination temperature: 68 to 86 degrees Fahrenheit; Growth temperature: 70 to 75 degrees Fahrenheit; Days to bloom: 55 to 75.
Uses: Back of border, drying, edible seeds.

Helichrysum bracteatum (hee-li-KRY-sum brak-tee-AH-tum) **strawflower,** HH, easy. 🌡 ❀ ○

Height: 16 inches for dwarf varieties, 3 feet for tall varieties.
Colors: White, yellow, pink, orange, red, gold, crimson, bicolor.
Characteristics: A popular everlasting flower for bright winter

bouquets. Strawflowers are available in a wide assortment of bold and unusual flower colors on compact-to-bushy plants. The double, daisylike flowers are practically dry on the plant. They hold their bright colors when dried. The flowers have the texture of paper or straw, thus the common name. *Helichrysum* is really a perennial from Australia that flowers easily from seed the first year.
Cultural Information: Prefers average, well-drained soils and despises too-rich or too-wet soils. Can be direct sown or started indoors for a longer period of bloom and harvest. Once established, the plants can withstand temperatures in the high twenties Fahrenheit.

To dry strawflowers, cut them before the center petals open and their pollen shows. Remove any foliage and wire the stems if you want them to be easier to handle. Follow the directions on page 93 for the best results. Space 10 to 12 inches apart.
Days to germinate: 8 to 21; Germination temperature: 70 to 75 degrees Fahrenheit; Growth temperature: 60 to 65 degrees Fahrenheit; Days to bloom: 50 to 85; Weeks to start indoors: 6 to 8.
Uses: Drying, edging, bedding, cutting.

Heliotropium (he-li-o-TRO-pee-um) **common heliotrope,** T, Native American, moderately easy. ❀ ○ ◑

Height: 15 inches for dwarf varieties, 4 feet for tall varieties.
Colors: Dark purple.
Characteristics: The common heliotrope varieties are old-

fashioned flowers cherished for their vanilla fragrance. The clusters of dark purple flowers are used in perfume-making. Heliotropes are really tender perennials from Peru that are more commonly grown as annuals, blooming from seed the first season. Plants can be cut back, potted up, and moved indoors for winter blooms but they must have moist air, direct sun, and cool nights of 50 to 55 degrees Fahrenheit.

'Marine', a dwarf variety (15 inches) with little fragrance but large flowers, bushy habit, and long bloom, is the most popular variety grown and the one most available. Grow *H. arborescens* for its fragrance.

Cultural Information: They like evenly moist, rich, well-drained soil. They can be grown from seeds, purchased as started plants, or grown from stem cuttings. Space dwarf varieties 8 to 10 inches apart and tall varieties 2 to 3 feet apart.

Days to germinate: 7 to 21; Germination temperature: 70 to 80 degrees Fahrenheit; Growth temperature: 65 to 70 degrees Fahrenheit; Days to bloom: about 90; Weeks to start indoors: 10 to 12.

Uses: Bedding, cutting, and houseplant.

Hyacinth bean; see Annual Vines: *Dolichos*

Hypoestes (hi-po-ES-teez) **polka-dot plant,** HH, moderate. ○ ◖

Height: 12 inches.

Colors: Deep green foliage spotted with pink, small lilac flowers.

Characteristics: This plant is grown for its unusual foliage

color. The leaves are dark green and appear to be splashed with pink paint. It is traditionally grown as a houseplant but is unusual and well-behaved in a border. If planted next to pink snapdragons, it mirrors their color. I plant it as a groundcover in a woodland setting next to violas.

'Pink Splash', 'Confetti', 'Wine Red' are all handsome varieties, depending on which colors you prefer.

Cultural Information: This plant prefers average garden soil with excellent drainage. Fertilizer is not needed when planted outdoors; when grown as a houseplant, it needs to be fertilized every two weeks during the growing season. It also likes a rich soil mixture and high humidity when grown as a houseplant. Let the top half of the soil dry out between watering. It must have a brief rest period in winter when they are not fertilized and watered sparingly. It can be started any time indoors. Space outdoor plantings 8 to 10 inches apart.

Days to germinate: 3 to 4; Germination temperature: 70 to 75 degrees Fahrenheit; Growth temperature: 70 to 75 degrees Fahrenheit; Days to bloom 70 to 84; Weeks to start indoors: 6 to 8.

Uses: Containers, border, groundcover, houseplant.

Iberis amara (eye-BEER-is a-MAH-ra), *Iberis umbellata* (eye-BEER-is um-bel-LAH-ta) **globe candytuft, rocket candytuft,** H, moderately easy. ✳ ◗ ○

Height: 8 inches.

Colors: Pink, rose, carmine, crimson, lavender, purple, white.

Top: Hypoestes 'Pink Splash'
Above: Iberis umbellata

Characteristics: Dark green foliage is topped with full, round, delicate flowers. Uniformly compact plants that are profuse bloomers make iberis ideal as an edger or at the front of the border.

Cultural Information: Candytuft will adapt to most climates but prefers to grow where summers are cool. Deadhead to encourage more bloom. Make sure plants are well-watered during

Right: Impatiens
wallerana *'Rosette
Hybrid'*
Far right: Impatiens
'New Guinea'

Above: Impatiens
'Dazzler Mix'
Right: Impatiens
wallerana *'Super Elfin®
Scarlet'*

periods of prolonged hot, dry weather. Sow seed outdoors late fall or early spring, as soon as the soil can be worked, as they do not transplant easily. Space 6 to 9 inches apart.

Days to germinate: 14 to 21; Germination temperature: 60 to 65 degrees Fahrenheit: Growth temperature: 50 to 55 degrees Fahrenheit: Days to bloom: about 60; Weeks before last frost to start indoors: 6 to 8.

Uses: Cutting, rock garden, edging, border.

Impatiens wallerana

(im-PAY-shee-ens wo-la-RAH-na) **busy lizzy; patient plant,** ✽ ○ ◐, T; ***I. balsamina,*** (bal-SAM-ee-na) **garden balsam, touch-me-not,** T; ✽ ○ ◐ ***I. Schlechteri*** (SHLEK-ter-i) **New Guinea impatiens, T** ✽ ○, all easy bedding plants; *I. wallerana* and New Guinea impatiens, slightly challenging to grow from seed.

Height: 6 to 24 inches.

Colors: All colors and bicolors.

Characteristics: The impatiens name describes the seed pods that impatiently burst open when lightly touched, shooting the seed around the plant. (A fun activity for a child.)

Nothing can beat *I. wallerana* for brilliant summer-to-fall bloom in shady beds, borders, and containers. The hybrid varieties have longer bloom, a wider array of colors and more uniform sizes, and a few have variegated foliage. These plants have many improvements from the original *I. wallerana* from Tanzania (tender perennials).

It blooms well in semishady sites, not caring whether summers are hot or cool. This is a good indoor pot plant.

'Rosette', my favorite, has double flowers that look like miniature roses. It usually comes in a mix that includes full doubles, semidoubles and some singles, in brilliant red, scarlet, rose, pink, orange, salmon, white, and red/white bicolors. 'Blitz' hybrids come in a wide variety of colors and are larger-flowered (2 inches across) on compact plants 14 to 16 inches high. 'Super Elfin' hybrids are dwarf, uniform, low, spreading plants 10 to 12 inches. The 'Dazzler' hybrids have the widest array of colors with 1¾-inch flowers, and are only 8 inches high. They don't need pinching to force them into a bushy habit.

I. balsamina is a very easy, old-fashioned annual with double or single flowers, some resembling those of camillias, blooming on tall, straight stalks. The plants can be from 10 inches to 3 feet tall. *Balsamina* self-sows so readily I found it almost a nuisance (the young seedlings are easy to remove from unwanted places). Although considered tender, it returns year after year in my Zone 7 garden.

New Guinea impatiens prefer sun and have larger flowers, but in all other ways, they resemble their cousins in their long bloom, bushy appearance, easy care and wide range of colors. Some varieties have dark burgundy or variegated foliage that sets off their flowers.

Cultural Information: All species like rich, well-drained soil with plenty of moisture during dry periods.

I. wallerana will tolerate full sun if given plenty of water. Use slow-release fertilizers (low in nitrogen) to provide nutrients during the entire growing season. Reseeds readily in southern zones. Sow indoors anytime for houseplants.

Impatiens are easy to propagate from cuttings. If growing from seed, remember they need a minimum temperature of 70 degrees Fahrenheit to germinate. New Guinea impatiens are most successfully propagated by cuttings. 'Tango', an AAS-winner with big, bold, orange flowers 2 inches or more across, is an easy variety to grow from seed. Space all types 8 to 12 inches apart.

Days to germinate: 10 to 18; Germination temperature: 70 to 75 degrees Fahrenheit: Growth temperature: 60 to 65 degrees Fahrenheit; Days to Bloom: 53 to 75; Weeks to start indoors: 8. *Uses:* Edging, border, groundcover, container, hanging basket.

Kiss-me-over-the-garden-gate; see ***Amaranthus***

Larkspur; see ***Consolida***

Lathyrus odoratus (LA-thi-rus o-do-RAH-tus) **sweet pea,** H, difficult. ✳ 🌡 ❀ ○ ◑

Height: 9 to 15 inches for dwarf varieties, 5 to 6 feet for tall varieties.

Colors: All colors except yellow.

Characteristics: The delicate airy blossoms of sweet pea, shaped like miniature sunbonnets, can be single colors, bicolors, mottled, or striped. The colors themselves can be pale, soft tints or solid, deep colors. At the turn of the century, this plant was Burpee's best-selling annual and graced many a catalog cover. Flowers with longer blooming seasons and greater adaptability have surpassed it in popularity, but it deserves to be grown for its sweet fragrance and the beauty of its graceful, curving vines covered with delicate, old-fashioned flowers.

Use climbing sweet peas on fences, trellises, netting, or with supports growing up the side of a building. The bush types are good for edging, borders, and window boxes.

In addition to their beauty, sweet peas have had their impact on science. They are the plants with which Gregor Mendel conducted his experiments, founding the science of genetics.

Dwarf varieties are Burpee's 'Patio' and 'Bijou'. Neither of these bushy plants needs staking. Patio has larger flowers, but 'Bijou' blooms earlier and longer. Tall, vining varieties that need support for their tendrils to climb are 'Early Multiflora Gigantea', an early-blooming, heat-resistant variety, and Burpee's 'Galaxy', a multiflowered climber with bloom from early summer on. Many stems have five or more large flowers.

Cultural Information: Sweet peas like well-drained neutral-to-lime soil, rich in humus. Plant in spring as early as soil can be prepared. Sweet peas do best where weather is cool.

Soak seed in lukewarm water overnight or for 24 hours to soften the seed coat and speed germination. It is best to sprinkle Legume Aid® or Burpee Booster® on the soil where you place the seeds; these organic preparations put millions of live nitrogen-fixing bacteria into the soil, enabling the roots to use atmospheric nitrogen. This will improve growth and increase the number of flowers. Mulch to keep roots cool and water deeply and regularly. For earliest, best, and longest bloom in northern areas where spring quickly turns into hot summer, we recommend starting seeds indoors (in pots) late February or early March. After heavy frost but while weather is still cool, move the plants to a well-drained, sunny area.

Sweet peas can be sown outdoors in spring as early as the soil can be worked. In the South and Pacific Southwest, sweet peas are planted from fall to winter. Sweet peas are ideally suited for spring growth in the coastal regions of the Northwest and New England, and also do nicely in a cool greenhouse. Cut regularly for indoor bouquets to help extend the blooming

Lathyrus odoratus 'Royal'

Top: Lavatera
'Silver Cup'
Above: Limonium
sinuatum *'Mixed Colors'*

season. They do not like transplanting; sow where they are to grow or start indoors in peat pots to prevent root disturbance when transplanting. All parts of this plant are poisonous. Space 6 inches apart, depending on variety.

Days to germinate: 14 to 20; Germination temperature: 55 degrees Fahrenheit; Growth temperature: 50 to 60 degrees Fahrenheit: Days to bloom: 80 to 90; Weeks to start indoors be-

fore outdoor planting is possible: 6 to 8.
Uses: Edging, border, cutting, container.

Lavatera (lah-va-TEE-ra) **mallow,** H, moderately easy.

🌡 ❀ ○

Height: 2 to 4 feet.
Colors: Pink.
Characteristics: Glowing pink, single hollyhocklike flowers up to 3 inches across are free-blooming (don't need deadheading) and make a quick-growing summer hedge or screen. The bushy plants have dark green, maple-leaflike foliage and hairy stems.

'Silver Cup' is a European award-winner for its long bloom and bushy habit. Plants are 24 inches to 30 inches high.
Cultural Information: The plants prefer a light-to-ordinary but well-drained soil. Best to sow in the garden where it is to grow, as it doesn't like transplanting. They can be sown in the fall or as early as the soil can be worked in the spring.

If starting indoors, plant in peat pots where the roots will not be disturbed in transplanting. When grown indoors, allow the plants to dry out between watering. *Lavatera* do not like hot weather. Cut flowers are lovely but short-lived. Plants rarely require staking. Space 15 to 24 inches apart.
Days to germinate: 15 to 21; Germination temperature: 70 degrees Fahrenheit; Growth temperature: 50 to 55 degrees Fahrenheit; Days to bloom: about 90; Weeks to start indoors: 6 to 8.
Uses: Background, border, cutting, greenhouse.

Limonium sinuatum (lee-MO-nee-um sin-ew-AH-tum) **statice,** HH, moderately easy.

💧 ☀ 🌡 ○

Height: 2½ feet.
Colors: White, yellow, pink, rose, blue, lavender, apricot.
Characteristics: One of the most popular and best everlasting flowers for indoor winter bouquets. The papery texture of the flowers holds the colors as they practically dry on the plant. Varieties are available in a wide range of colors, from soft pastels to bright, bold colors, some so unusual as to appear almost artificial. They can be used fresh as well as dry.
Cultural Information: This plant tolerates heat, drought, salt spray, and almost any soil except clay. Prefers conditions on the dry side; too much water causes root rot. Continued cutting encourages additional flowering stems to develop. Easy to dry (follow the simple directions on page 93). In Florida, commercial growers sow seed by the acre in midsummer for harvest in midwinter for dried bouquets and wreaths. Space plants 9 inches apart.

Difficult to transplant because of its long taproot.
Days to germinate: 14 to 21; Germination temperature: 70 degrees Fahrenheit; Growth temperature: 75+ degrees Fahrenheit; Days to bloom: 75 to 90; Weeks before last frost to start indoors: 8 to 10.
Uses: Cutting, drying, border.

Lisianthus; see *Eustoma*

Lobelia erinus (lo-BELL-ee-a E-ri-nus) HH, moderate.

❀ ◑ ○

Height: Dwarf varieties 4 to 5 inches, trailing varieties 4 inches.
Colors: White, rose, blue, violet, some with white eyes.
Characteristics: Compact plants with small-lipped flowers and green-to-bronze leaves. Some varieties are wonderful for draping over the edges and down the sides of containers and window boxes. Lobelia 'Sapphire' is a trailing variety that is charming with its dark blue flowers accented by a white eye. The dwarf varieties make good edgings, and all varieties are suited to planting in a rock garden. 'Blue Moon' is a delicate edging for a bed of white impatiens and an excellent choice for southern gardens where it stands up well to prolonged high temperatures.
Cultural Information: This plant takes part shade where summer is hot, full sun in cooler areas. It likes average to rich soil and should be sheared back to 2 inches after the first blooms start to fade to help it continue flowering. It is short-lived, but often self-sows. It may stop flowering if summers are too hot, and doesn't thrive where temperatures and humidity are high. When starting indoors, keep the slow-growing seedlings evenly moist until the plants are established. The seed is very fine and should not be covered because it needs light to germinate. In areas where summers are hot, give them some shade. It can be propagated in the fall from cuttings for indoor winter bloom on a sunny window. The plants are poisonous and should not be eaten. Space plants 6 inches apart.

Days to germinate: 20; Germination temperature: 70 to 80 degrees Fahrenheit; Growth temperature: 60 to 65 degrees Fahrenheit; Days to bloom: 75 to 100; Weeks to start indoors: 8 to 12.
Uses: Container, edging.

Lobularia maritima (lob-yew-LAH-ree-a ma-RI-ti-ma) **sweet alyssum,** H, easy. ✳ ❀ ○ ◖

Height: 3 to 4 inches.
Colors: White, pinks, blue, violet, deep rose, reddish rose.
Characteristics: Tiny, delicate flowers cover this wonderfully fragrant plant from late spring to hard frost. Mature alyssum spreads several times its height. It is a perennial native to southern Europe and is a good garden plant, performing well even when summers are very hot. It can be grown in the crevices of stone paths or stone walls.

Plant it as an edger in a window box and its fragrance will drift into the house with the summer breezes.
Cultural Information: This plant is quick to germinate and early to flower. It can be direct sown outdoors where it is to grow as soon as there is no danger of heavy frost; there is no advantage to starting seeds indoors. Simply scatter seeds on a prepared bed and don't cover them. The plant will frequently reseed itself for abundant flowers the following year.

When it starts to slow its bloom, cut off flowers and it will bloom all summer. Most books tell you to shear the tops, but that gives the plant a shaved, unnatural look that takes several weeks to outgrow. If you have a small area, use scissors and give a more natural, less even cut. Fertilize and it will grow back sooner and continue to flower until heavy frost. Space plants 6 inches apart.

Days to germinate: 5 to 10; Germination temperature: 70 degrees Fahrenheit; Growth temperature: 50 to 60 degrees Fahrenheit; Days to bloom: 40 to 60; Weeks to start indoors: 4 to 6.
Uses: Edging, container, houseplant, groundcover.

Love-in-a-mist; see *Nigella*

Love-lies-bleeding; see *Amaranthus*

Mallow; see *Lavatera*

Marigold; see *Tagetes*

Top: Lobelia erinus 'String of Pearls Mixed'
Above: Lobularia maritima 'Color Carpet'

Top: Matthiola incana 'Giant Imperial Mixed'
Center: Mirabilis 'Jingles'
Bottom: Mimulus species 'Malibu Hybrid Mixed'

Matthiola incana (ma-tee-O-la in-KAH-na) **stock,** HH, moderate. ✳ 🌡 🎟 ○

Height: 15 to 30 inches.

Colors: White, pink, rose, lavender.

Characteristics: Another old-fashioned flower that produces heavy spikes of sweet-spicy smelling flowers. It has fallen from favor probably because it loves cool weather and will actually stop blooming in hot weather. The blue-gray foliage is attractive even without flowers, but the plant will resume blooming when the weather cools down. It can be grown as a houseplant with temperatures no higher than 65 degrees Fahrenheit for blooming.

'Trysomic Seven Week' varieties—a breeder breakthrough—are the earliest to bloom (seven weeks), bearing mostly double flowers; does well where temperatures are hot and other stocks are difficult to grow.

Stock is a perennial in southern Europe where it is native.

Cultural Information: This plant thrives in cool weather and likes a porous, loose, moist soil. Buds won't set on most stock varieties if temperatures are above 65 degrees Fahrenheit for more than six hours a day. Regular liquid feeding is helpful as stocks have a high potash requirement; a deficiency is evident by a brown "burning" on the edges of older leaves. Space dwarf plants 8 inches apart and taller plants 16 inches.

Days to germinate: 10 to 20; Germination temperature: 65 to 70 degrees Fahrenheit; Growth temperature: 50 to 60 degrees Fahrenheit (likes 50-degree nights); Days to bloom: 65 to 85; Weeks before last heavy frost to start indoors: 6 to 8.

Uses: Cutting, border.

Mexican sunflower; see **Tithonia**

Mimulus (MIM-yew-lus) **monkey flower,** HH, Native American, easy. ✳ 🎟 ◑

Height: 10 inches.

Colors: Orange, yellow, red mixtures.

Characteristics: Mounded plants with quick-blooming, tubular flowers that are blotched and spotted in every conceivable manner, reminding one of the playful faces of monkeys.

This plant is ideally planted next to a stream, where it will get plenty of water. A tender perennial in Zones 9 and 10 (see The USDA Plant Hardiness Map, page 00), grown as a half-hardy annual in other zones. Plants can be brought indoors for winter bloom. To prolong bloom period, remove all faded flowers.

Cultural Information: Prefers cool weather and needs lots of water. Likes a rich, moist, well-drained soil. Barely cover seeds with soil when planting. Space 6 inches apart.

Days to germinate: 7 to 14; Germination temperature: 60 to 70 degrees Fahrenheit; Growth temperature: 55 to 60 degrees Fahrenheit; Days to bloom: 60; Weeks before last frost to start indoors: 8 to 12.

Uses: Groundcover, edging, houseplant, hanging basket.

Mirabilis (mee-RAH-bi-lis) **four o'clock,** H, easy. 💧 ✺ ○ ◑

Height: 2½ to 3 feet.
Colors: White, yellow, rose, red, bicolors.
Characteristics: Each plant has flowers of many different colors and many different color combinations. The flowers open late in the day, around four o'clock, and remain open all night and into the next day, closing in bright sun to protect themselves from scorching. On cloudy days, when we all need a lift, they are in full bloom.

Another old-fashioned tender perennial for frost-free areas. *Mirabilis* sprout readily and bloom profusely—very rewarding for a child's garden. They also tolerate dust, soot, fumes and other pollutants, making them a perfect choice for the city garden. They reseed themselves with enthusiasm and are very attractive to hummingbirds.
Cultural Information: This plant takes heat, drought, poor or sandy soil. However, it will appreciate good soil and occasional feeding. Its roots form tubers that can be dug up in the fall and saved like those of dahlias and begonias for planting again the next spring. Space plants 14 inches apart.
Days to germinate: 10 to 14; Germination temperature: 70 to 80 degrees Fahrenheit; Growth temperature: 60 to 65 degrees Fahrenheit; Days to bloom: 60 to 85; Weeks to start indoors: 4 to 6.
Uses: Bedding, container.

Moluccella (mo-lu-KEL-la) bells of Ireland, HH, moderate. 🌢 ○ ◑
Height: 2 to 3 feet.
Colors: Apple green bracts with tiny white flowers.

Characteristics: Bells of Ireland is grown for its light apple green, bell-shaped bracts that line the stem. Tucked deep in each bract is a tiny, white, fragrant flower. Aside from their fragrance, the flowers are insignificant and drop as plants mature. This plant is slow-growing and matures in late summer.

The flowers are attractive for both fresh and dried arrangements if you pull off the small leaves that grow between the bracts, exposing their bell shape. This plant did not originate in Ireland but was named for being the favorite color of the Irish.
Cultural Information: This plant likes good drainage and average soil. The hardest part of growing Bells of Ireland is germinating the seed; oddly enough, the seed coat contains a strong inhibitor to seed germination. It is best to chill the seeds for five days in the refrigerator (50 degrees Fahrenheit), then soak them overnight in lukewarm water to soften and remove the hard seed coat. Softening or removal of the seed coat increases the percentage of seeds that will germinate. When planting, don't cover the seeds as they need light to germinate. It is best to direct sow after all danger of frost and before the weather turns hot and impedes germination. The plant will self-sow in favorable locations. It is easy to transplant if you are careful to dig deep enough to get the whole taproot.

If growing for drying, follow the directions on page 93. The bells will turn straw color when dry. Space plants 12 inches apart.
Days to germinate: 10 to 21;

Molucella laevis

Germination temperature: 60 to 85 degrees Fahrenheit; Growth temperature: 70+ degrees Fahrenheit; Days to bloom: 90; Weeks start indoors before last frost: 8.
Uses: Cutting, garden border.

Monkey flower; see ***Mimulus***

Moonflower; see Annual Vines: ***Ipomoea***

Morning bride; see ***Scabiosa***

Morning glory; see ***Ipomoea***

Moss rose; see ***Portulaca***

Top: Myosotis
sylvatica *'Blue Bird'*
Above: Nicotiana alata
'Nicki Hybrid Mixed'

Myosotis sylvatica (mee-os-O-tus sil-VA-ti-ka) **forget-me-not,** H, easy. ◗ ◐ ○
Height: 7 to 12 inches.
Colors: Bright blue, pink, white.
Characteristics: One of the finest spring flowers, forget-me-not performs best when given some shade, and is lovely naturalized in woodlands, where it reseeds itself. Plant seeds in the fall over tulips, and come spring you'll have tulips blooming in a sea of blue forget-me-nots. They are long-lasting cut flowers for spring bouquets.
Cultural Information: This is a good plant for wet conditions; this means additional water is required during long periods of hot, dry weather. Seeds need darkness for germination. The plant will stay in bloom longer if it is not allowed to go to seed. Seed can be sown in the fall, over the spot where spring-blooming bulbs have been planted, started early indoors, or directly sown outdoors early in the spring. Space individual plants 6 inches apart.
Days to germinate: 8 to 14; Germination temperature: 65 to 70 degrees Fahrenheit; Growth temperature: 70+ degrees Fahrenheit: Days to bloom: 90; Weeks to start indoors: 8 to 12; Plant out 4 to 6 weeks before last frost.
Uses: Edging, bedding, cutting, groundcover.

Nasturtium; see ***Tropaeolum***

New Guinea impatiens; see ***Impatiens***

Nicotiana (nee-Ko-tee-AH-na) **flowering tobacco,** HH, Native American from Brazil, moderately easy. ◗ ❀ ○ ◐
Height: 1½ to 4 feet.
Colors: White, pink, rose, red, purple, wine.
Characteristics: Profuse, star-shaped trumpet flowers and broad, light green leaves make this a good middle- or back-of-the-border plant. A member of the same family that provides the leaves for tobacco.

The old favorite years ago, *Nicotiana sylvestris* was grown for its wonderful fragrance (strongest at night), but it fell from favor because it required staking. Dwarf versions of *Nicotiana alata*, the Nicky hybrid, for example, are better behaved. They don't need staking and have wonderful color and long bloom (but little fragrance).

These plants are perennials in Zone 10 (see The USDA Plant Hardiness Map, page 94). The newer hybrids stay open during the day while the old-fashioned, open-pollinated varieties close in cloudy weather.

Nicky hybrids come in a wide assortment of colors and are attractive, self-branching, free flowering, versatile semidwarf (height 16 to 18 inches) varieties, with the old-fashioned star-shaped, tubular flowers that bloom all season.
Cultural Information: Easy to direct sow, but seeds are very fine. Use a garden blanket to keep seeds from washing away in heavy rains. Don't cover the seeds with soil, as they need light to germinate. If not growing under lights, do not sow before March 1, as the plant needs long days to bloom. Prefers a good garden soil with lots of organic matter. During periods of prolonged hot, dry weather, additional moisture may be needed. Thrives in humid areas but suffers in the prolonged hot, humid conditions of southern gardens, where it is best grown

as a spring/early summer flower discarded when it starts to look ragged. Prefers average to rich, moist and well-drained soil. Space 9 inches apart for dwarf varieties and up to 2 feet for taller varieties.

Days to germinate: 10 to 12; Germination temperature: 70 degrees Fahrenheit; Growth temperature: 70+ degrees Fahrenheit; Days to bloom: 55 to 65; Weeks to start indoors before last frost: 6 to 8.

Uses: Borders, container, cutting.

Nierembergia caerulea

(nee-e-ram-BERG-ee-a ka-RU-lee-a) **cupflower,** T, Native American, easy. ✳ ❀ ○ ◗

Height: 6 inches.
Colors: Violet-blue.
Characteristics: Vibrant, cup-shaped flowers bloom through the summer on plants 6 inches high. They are really tender perennial wildflowers from Argentina that bloom the first season from seed. They are inclined to sprawl or creep, which makes them good edgers.

'Purple Robe' (AAS-winner) is a dense, long-flowering variety valued in the rock garden.

Cultural Information: Ordinary garden soil to rich, light, moist, well-drained soil. They prefer a cool summer and should be shaded where summers are hot. They may need additional moisture during periods of prolonged hot, dry weather. Perennials in the South, they can be propagated by cuttings or division. In the North they can winter over in a greenhouse or cold frame. Space small plants 6 inches apart.

Days to germinate: 15 to 25; Germination temperature: 70 to 75 degrees Fahrenheit; Growth temperature: 70+ degrees Fahrenheit; Days to bloom: 50 to 65; Weeks to start indoors: 8 to 10.

Uses: Edging, rock garden, container, hanging basket, window box.

Nigella damascena (ny-JELL-a dam-a-SKAY-na) **love-in-a-mist,** H, moderately easy. ▮ ○

Height: 18 inches.
Colors: White, pink, red, purple.
Characteristics: Rounded, cornflowerlike flowers surrounded by ferny, threadlike foliage which makes the plant appear as though in a mist, hence the name. This is an old-fashioned flower that deserves to be better known today. Dried seed heads and dried flowers can both be used for winter bouquets.

Cultural Information: Any well-drained soil supplemented with lime. Fertilize monthly with a light application of 5–10–5. Since it resents transplanting, it is best to sow where it is to grow. Reseeds itself readily for the following year. Blooms approximately four weeks, leaving attractive seed pods. To keep flowers blooming all summer, plan successive sowings. Seeds can be sown outdoors in the fall or spring. Space 6 to 8 inches apart.

Days to germinate: 21; Germination temperature: 60 degrees Fahrenheit; Growth temperature: 70+ degrees Fahrenheit; Days to bloom: 105.

Uses: Border, cutting, dried.

Painted tongue; see *Salpiglossis*

Pansy; see *Viola*

Top: Nigella damascena
Above: Nierembergia
'Purple Robe'

Papaver rhoeas (pa-PAH-ver RO-as) **Shirley poppy, corn poppy,** H, easy. ✳ ○
Height: 18 inches.
Colors: Yellow, pink, scarlet, crimson, salmon, white.
Characteristics: Lovely for midsummer bloom, the delicate, crinkled flowers are nearly translucent and come in single, semidouble, and double blossoms that bloom in many colors. These poppies are excellent cut flowers. If happy, they return year after year to grace your garden.
Cultural Information: They like rich, well-drained soil where they can be direct sown to remain in the garden; they don't transplant well. Successive sowings give best results. The seeds are very tiny, so be careful when opening the package that you don't pour them all in one spot. This plant likes cool climates. Sow seeds in the fall except where winters are very severe; then, sow in early spring. They reseed readily, but for longer flowering, pick off dead blooms.

If using for a cut flower, first seal the end of the stem in boiling water or with a lighted match to prevent the milky sap from clogging the stem. Space 6 to 8 inches apart.
Days to germinate: 8 to 15; Germination temperature: 55 to 60 degrees Fahrenheit; Growth temperature: 70+ degrees Fahrenheit; Days to bloom: 80.
Uses: Middle of the border, rock garden, cutting.

Patient plant; see ***Impatiens***

Pelargonium (pel-ar-GO-ni-um) **geranium,** T, easy, if using scarified seed (scratch or make a shallow cut in the seed coat, or purchase seed treated with a germination enhancer). 🌡 ❀ ○ ◐
Height: 12 to 20 inches.
Colors: White, red, pink, purple, salmon, carmine, orange, scarlet.
Characteristics: Geraniums are probably America's most popular flower. The standard red geranium that brightens window boxes and gardens across America performs well in spite of all the demands of city life: pollution, smog, dust and partial shade. These plants are perennial in frost-free areas, growing to 4 or 5 feet tall and looking more like shrubs. They can be saved in a dormant condition in northern climates, for renewed blooming the following years.

Everyone is familiar with the full, round blossoms and many colors of standard geraniums, and the long vines and open flowers of the ivy geraniums. The old-fashioned scented geraniums, sold as herbs, are not as well known, and they should be. They were very popular at the turn of the century as plants for a sunny window, releasing their fragrance when touched. Probably their lack of popularity is because they are not as profuse in their bloom, showing smaller, more delicate, and open flowers. As fragrant foliage plants they are unbeatable, available with many styles of leaves from crimped, ruffled or curled, to deeply cut or broad, velvety or rough. The best part is the fabulous variety of fragrances that run from lemon, rose, apple, cinnamon and wintergreen to "light champagne." For fragrance, grow scented geraniums.

The white-edged leaves of 'Snowflake' are so attractive that it's worth growing for its foliage alone, but it brings with it a lemon-rose fragrance, an added gift.

The red- and yellow-rimmed leaves of zonal geraniums look hand-painted and remind me of Imari china. The foliage even without a flower is wonderful for cutting and using in arrangements or floating in a bowl.

'Summer Showers' is an ivy-leaf geranium that can be grown from seed. 'Pinto' is an early-blooming, 16-inch plant with zoned (two-color) foliage, and 'Elite' is a compact plant 12 to 14 inches tall, topped with large, 4-inch flower heads that are early to bloom.

Cultural Information: Sow seed indoors, in a cold frame or greenhouse, 10 to 12 weeks before last heavy frost. Transplant to large pots; or set in a sunny garden after heavy frost. They prefer average, well-drained soil. In frost-free areas, geraniums are perennial; sow fall to early spring. For houseplants, sow anytime. Young plants must not dry out, but established plants are not demanding. For best results, fertilize every 3 to 4 weeks with 5–10–5 to improve the quality of blooms.

Geraniums are easy to propagate from cuttings, especially the scented and ivy types, which are difficult to grow from seed. The cuttings usually root in four weeks or less, especially if a root-inducing additive is used. Sterile sand is best as a rooting medium. Space 10 to 12 inches apart.

Days to germinate: 7 to 21; Germination temperature: 70 to 75 degrees Fahrenheit; Growth temperature: 70 + degrees Fahrenheit; Days to bloom: 100; Weeks before last frost to start indoors: 10 to 12.

Uses: Container, window box, flowerbed, border.

Perilla (pe-RIL-la) **beefsteak plant,** HH, moderately easy. ✳ ○ ◖

Height: 3 feet.

Colors: Deep purple-red foliage, insignificant white, reddish, or violet flowers.

Characteristics: A tall member of the basil family with dark, handsome foliage of a purple-red sheen. This old-fashioned herb has been rediscovered, and is used more and more as an ornamental at the back of borders to add color and set off the shorter annuals toward the front. Late in the season, short spikes of white, reddish, or violet flowers appear.

Leaves and seeds are used in tempura. The seeds are salted in Japan and served after sweets, and the dried seed pods are very attractive in flower arrangements.

Cultural Information: Readily re-seeds and could become a pest except that it is very easy to pull out and give to friends or transplant. However, when it is transplanted and especially if the roots are disturbed, it will stop growing for a time. It needs light to germinate. Pinch back to induce bushiness. It is easy to propagate from cuttings. Space 12 inches apart.

Days to Germinate: 8 to 14; Germination temperature: 65 to 75; Growth temperature: 75; days to bloom: 50 to 60; Weeks to start indoors: 4 to 6.

Uses: Cutting, back of border.

Above: Perilla
*Left: Double grandiflora
Petunia x hybrida
'Purple Pirouette'
Opposite, from top:
Papaver rhoeas
'Double-Flowered
Mixed'; Pelargonium
zonale 'Summer
Showers Hybrid';
Pelargonium zonale
'Earliana Mixed'.*

Periwinkle; see ***Catharanthus***

Petunia (pe-TEWN-ee-a) HH, Native American from Argentina, moderate. 🌡 ✿ ○

Height: 12 to 16 inches.

Colors: White, yellows, corals, pinks, reds, blues, purples, and bicolors.

VERSATILE F₁ HYBRID PETUNIAS FOR EVERY TYPE OF CONTAINER OR GARDEN ARRANGEMENT

TYPE	Single Grandiflora		Double Grandiflora	Single Floribunda	Single Multiflora	Double Multiflora
VARIETY	Supercascade Series	Daddy Series, Flash Series, Falcon Series, Happiness, Supermagic Series, Ultra Series	Ball All-Double Mixture, Circus, Double Sure, Fanfare Mixture, Purple Pirouette, Sonata	Madness Series	Comanche, Sugar Plum, Summer Sun	Tart Series, Delight Series
FLOWER SIZE	3½ to 5 in.	3 to 4 in.	3 to 4 in.	2 to 3 in.	1½ to 2 in.	2 in.
SPACING	10 in.	10 in.	10 in.	10 in.	10 in.	10 in.
USE	Bedding, tubs, hanging baskets	Mass plantings, bedding	Porch boxes, tubs	Mass plantings, bedding	Mass plantings, bedding	Porch boxes
COMMENTS	The largest-selling type		Unique double type	Most disease/weather tolerant	Prolific bloomer	Popular novelty

Single grandiflora
Petunia x hybrida
'Flair'

Characteristics: The petunia is one of those fragrant, old-fashioned flowers that has never lost its popularity; instead it has just gotten better and better. These plants are reliable, versatile, and easily adaptable. Individual flower sizes range from 2 to 5 inches across and can be single or double, plain, or fringed; the plants can be cascading or upright. All have abundant bloom.

There are many petunias from which to choose, depending on color, flower size, and personal taste. The varieties that follow are my favorites. The Madness series, so called because "they flower like mad," are large-flowered (3 inches, some veined with contrasting colors), prolific bloomers with good garden performance and weather tolerance. A good choice for the heat of the Southeast is 'Summer Madness', a coral with rose veins. This is a personal favorite, the petunia always admired by visitors to my garden. The Americana series plants are wonderful for bright, clear, solid colors. They are bushy 12-inch plants that bloom all summer, require no deadheading, and show remarkable rain tolerance.

Hybrid varieties are somewhat more expensive than standard petunias because they are hand-pollinated. For that extra charge, you buy more unusual flowers with more color combinations, larger size and enhanced weather resistance. One goal for petunia breeders is flowers that can stand up to heavy rains and keep smiling; both the American series (AAS-winner) and the Madness series, among others, have these qualities. When you're putting all this effort into growing, it makes sense to buy the hybrid petunias. *Cultural Information:* Established plants will grow in a wide range of soils but prefer fertile loam or light, sandy soil with good drainage. Commercial growers have found, while growing seedlings for transplanting, that weekly feeding and maintaining a temperature of 60 degrees Fahrenheit brings bloom several weeks early. If the foliage color becomes lighter green, lightly sprinkle 5–10–5 fertilizer around the stem, but not touching the plant. Petunias dry out quickly and need to be given ample water during hot weather. In warmer climates they can self-sow. The seeds are extremely small and need light to germinate. It is best to start indoors and to water from below to avoid moving and disrupting the tiny seeds. Cover them to keep them from drying out. Pinch back when petunias reach 6 inches to encourage bushiness. Over the summer any ungainly, drooping stems can be cut back to keep the plant neat and encourage more flowers. Cuttings can be taken in late summer to start pot plants for winter bloom. Space 8 to 12 inches apart.

Days to germinate: 10 to 12; Germination temperature: 70 to 80 degrees Fahrenheit; Growth temperature: 70+ degrees Fahrenheit; Days to bloom: 60 to 75; Weeks before last frost to start indoors: 10 to 12.

Uses: Edging, bedding, cutting, container.

Phlox drummondii (floks dru-MOND-ee-ee) **annual phlox, Texas pride,** HH, Native American from Texas, easy. ✽ 🌡 ❀ ○

Height: 6 to 8 inches for dwarf varieties, 15 to 18 inches for tall varieties.

Colors: Pink, salmon, red, purple, white, bicolor.

Characteristics: A compact and free-flowering, slightly fragrant annual that grows wild in Texas, loving hot southern summers. The medium green, smooth leaves are covered with clusters of single blooms. If you consistently pick off faded flowers, you can extend the bloom almost the entire summer.

Phlox is attractive planted as a groundcover around or in front of taller, barer-stemmed annuals or summer bulbs (gladiolus and abutilon, for example).

They are good cut flowers with a lovely fragrance.

Cultural Information: Thrives in any kind of soil, but prefers light, rich loam. What appear to be the weakest seedlings will often give the best color, so don't despair. Can be direct sown in the garden after danger of frost is past. Phlox are heavy feeders, so use an organic or slow-release (5–10–15) fertilizer and give the flowers a boost with liquid fertilizer once or twice a season.

These plants can be propagated by cuttings. Space 10 inches apart.

Days to germinate: 10 to 21; Germination temperature: 60 to 65 degrees Fahrenheit; Growth temperature: 70+ degrees Fahrenheit; Days to bloom: 60 to 70; Weeks to start indoors: 8.

Uses: Edging, bedding, rock garden, cutting, container.

Pincushion   flower; see *Scabiosa*

Pinks; see *Dianthus*

Plume thistle; see *Cirsium*

Poinsettia, annual; see *Euphorbia*

Poinsettia, summer; see *Amaranthus*

Polka-dot plant; see *Hypoestes*

Poor man's orchid; see *Schizanthus*

Poppy,   California; see *Eschscholzia*

Poppy, Shirley; see *Papaver*

Pot marigold; see *Calendula*

Portulaca grandiflora (por-twe-LAH-ka grand-i-FLO-ra) **moss rose or sun rose**, HH, Native American from Brazil, easy. 💧 ✽ ❀ ○

Height: 6 to 7 inches.

Colors: Bright and soft tones of all colors except blue.

Characteristics: This plant is the champion for survival in heat and drought, but also performs well where summers are cool and short. Needlelike, succulent light green leaves help it survive heat and drought well while forming a ground-hugging rug. Just a few plants can cover quite an area of ground, its spread being several times its height. The single or double flowers open during sunny days

Top: Phlox drummondi 'Petticoat Mixed'
Center: Phlox 'Dwarf Beauty Mixed'
Bottom: Portulaca grandiflora 'Magic Carpet®'

Top: Salpiglossis 'Casino Mix'
Above: Salvia splendens 'Carabiniere Scarlet'

would grow. It is the next of kin to "purley" or purslane, a most persistent, recurring weed, and a bane to gardeners everywhere.

Avoid excess watering but make sure the soil stays fairly moist during germination as only established plants can thrive in hot, dry conditions. Grows quickly from seed, which makes it easy to direct sow outdoors after the last frost date. The only danger is that the tiny seeds (they resemble iron filings) will wash away or be covered too deeply for germination. A garden blanket will help protect them from the elements, and they can be started indoors too. Thinning is not necessary as these plants love to be crowded. Days to germinate: 10 to 14; Germination temperature: 70 to 80 degrees Fahrenheit; Growth temperature: 70 to 75 degrees Fahrenheit; Days to bloom: 54 to 65; Weeks to start indoors: 8.
Uses: Rock garden, edging, container, border, groundcover.

Prairie gentian; see ***Eustoma***

Pyrethrum ptarmiciflorum; see ***Chrysanthemum***

Sage; see ***Salvia***

Salpiglossis (sal-pi-GLOSS-is) **velvet flower or painted tongue,** HH, Native American from Chile, moderate. ✴ 🌡 ❀ ○ ◑
Height: 2½ feet.
Colors: Bicolors and tricolors— gold, scarlet, maroon, blue, purple, yellow.
Characteristics: Mother Nature

and close on cloudy, overcast, and rainy days, as well as at night. Moss rose is wonderful for lining a path or growing between stones in hot, dry areas. The color combinations are usually strong, bold, primary colors. This plant readily reseeds when happy.
Cultural Information: Poor but well-drained soil suits this plant well, and its tiny seed will survive in the driest, most sun-struck places where few flowers

teaches us a lot about combining colors without clashing. Notice the unusual color combinations of this plant's flowers. One flower has a purple background veined with bright red and orange. The effect is beautiful and arresting. All of the velvety, large, funnel-shaped flowers of salpiglossis are veined or netted in intricate patterns with unusual and striking color combinations. They are slender, upright bushy plants with toothed, oblong leaves on long graceful stems. They are perennial in warm climates. Grow them for cutting and bring indoors where their colors can be admired at close range.
Cultural Information: Does best where summers are cool. This plant likes rich, light soil with excellent drainage. When growing indoors, sow the extremely fine seed in a peat pot in order to avoid disturbing the roots at transplanting. Even so, the plants may sulk after transplanting and take a little time to recover from the shock. *Salpiglossis* are slow-growing only as small plants.

Outdoors, directly sow where the plants are to grow. The seeds need light, but like to be barely covered with soil. Keep soil evenly moist. Pinch out plant centers of young plants to help them branch. May need supports. Space 10 to 12 inches apart.
Days to germinate: 8 to 15; Germination temperature: 70 to 80 degrees Fahrenheit; Growth temperature: 70+ degrees Fahrenheit: Days to flower: 70 to 100; Weeks to start indoors: 8.
Uses: Background border, cutting, container.

Salvia (SAL-vee-a) **sage,** HH, Native American, moderate. 🌡 ❀ ○

Height: 7 to 24 inches.
Colors: Red, scarlet, pinks, white, and blue.
Characteristics: Salvias are members of the mint family. Our native American tender perennial, *Salvia farinacea*, has become a popular bedding plant across America because of its ease of growth, and its beautiful spikes of bright blue or white flowers. It grows wild in Texas and New Mexico from early summer to fall. With its persistent long bloom, it is valued as a cut flower for bouquets, and is easily dried for winter arrangements. It grows well even after a light frost and is resistant to disease.

There is another perennial variety from Brazil that is very popularly used as an annual, *S. splendens*. It is best known for its long spikes of scarlet blooms which attract hummingbirds. Another lesser known, tender perennial planted as an annual is *S. patens*. It has looser tubular and lipped flower forms in pastel colors—a very interesting and beautiful flower, especially for cutting, but it is not as floriferous, flowering less than other salvias. *S. horminum*, a true annual, also has looser and more open flower forms in rich violet-blue or soft pink with contrasting veins. Try some of the more unusual salvias. All of them are planted and treated as one-season annuals in northern climates and can be perennials in the South.

Dwarf varieties are the earliest to bloom but the taller varieties have more vigorous growth and often look better than dwarf varieties later in the season. 'Red Hot Sally' is an excellent dwarf variety of *S. splendens*, performing equally well in the high temperatures of the Southeast and the cool evenings of California. There are many good varieties on the market.

Cultural Information: In the South it is best to plant them in a partially shaded area to protect them from the scorching sun. Salvias perform best when well-watered and heavily fed. More watering may be needed during periods of hot dry weather.

Salvia seed is not hard to germinate if certain requirements are met, but it is also readily available as started plants. The planting soil needs to be thoroughly soaked before the seeds are sprinkled on top. Seeds should not be covered, but the container does need to be covered, to hold in moisture until the seeds germinate. It is best not to disturb the seeds by additional watering (unless necessary) until they germinate. A minimum temperature of 70 degrees Fahrenheit must be maintained at all times until the seeds sprout. Then, move them to a cooler place for growth and to prevent damp-off. In Zones 9 and 10 (see The USDA Plant Hardiness Map, page 94), seeds can be direct sown outdoors in late winter and early spring.

Winter-blooming houseplants can be propagated from cuttings in the fall. The roots of *S. farinacea* and *S. patens* can even be dug and stored in sand over the winter for spring replanting. Space plants 1 foot apart. Days to germinate: 12 to 15; Germination temperature: 70 to 80 degrees Fahrenheit; Growth temperature: 70+ degrees Fahrenheit; Days to bloom: 65 to 85; Weeks to start indoors: 8 to 10.
Uses: Cutting, drying, border, container.

Top left: Salvia splendens 'Carabiniere Purple'
Top right: Salvia farinacea 'Victoria'
Above: Scabiosa atropurpurea 'Giant Imperial'

Scabiosa atropurpurea (skab-ee-O-sa aht-ro-pur-PEWR-ee-a) **pincushion flower, morning bride,** *Scabiosa stellata* (ska-bi-O-sa ste-LAH-ta) **star flower,** HH, easy. 🌡 ❀ ○

Height: S. atropurpurea is ½ to 3 feet, *S. stellata* is 2 feet.
Colors: S. atropurpurea is white, pink, red, burgundy, blue, purple, *S. stellata* is blue to rose-violet.

Above: Schizanthus
x wisetonensis 'Angel
Wings'

Opposite, from top:
Tagetes erecta
'Snowbird'; *Dwarf
single* Tagetes
patula 'Red Marietta';
Tagetes erecta 'Nugget
Hybrid Mixed'; *bottom
left,* Tagetes signata
pumila 'Golden Gem'
and 'Lemon Gem';
bottom right, Tagetes
patula 'Queen
Sophia®'.

Characteristics: Scabiosa stellata has double cushion or pincushionlike flowers that bloom on slender stems. There are many light-colored stamens, stuck like pins among the contrasting darker colored petals. Finely cut, lyre-shaped leaves grow in a whorl beneath the flowers. The plant is wonderful and delicate in bouquets as well as when mass-planted in the garden. To be noticed and admired, it must be planted in larger clumps. The effort of mass planting is worthwhile. A cool-temperature plant, it does better where the summers are moderate.

The seed pods resemble bottle-brushes and are intriguing when dried, adding interest to winter bouquets.

'Giant Imperial Mixed' is a good variety with fully double, ball-shaped blooms 2½ to 3 inches across. The plant is 3 feet high.

S. stellata is grown for its fascinating seed pods, light brown balls of little florets, each with a dark, spiny, starlike center; the flowers are small and insignificant. The seed pods grow up to 1½ inches across

and are an attractive addition to dried flower arrangements. Cut seed pods for drying when they are light brown in color and before they begin to shatter. Stems are strong and dry stiffly, making them easy to work with for winter bouquets. Children can paint the flower heads for Christmas tree ornaments.

Cultural Information: This plant likes rich, ordinary soil with excellent drainage, although it prefers an alkaline soil. Water it freely during dry weather. Remove faded flowers to extend their bloom. I direct sow in May, for cutting August through November. The plant continues to bloom even after a light frost, if it has not been allowed to go to seed. It can be fall sown where winters are mild. Sow the seeds closely together, 6 to 9 inches, and the plants will hold each other up.

Days to germinate: 12 to 21; *Germination temperature:* 65 to 70 degrees Fahrenheit; *Growth temperature:* 70 to 75 degrees Fahrenheit; *Days to bloom:* 90 to 120; *Weeks to start indoors:* 4 to 5.

Uses: Back of the border, cutting, and *S. stellata* for drying.

Schizanthus × *wisetonensis* (skiz-ANTH-us wiez-ton-EN-sis) **butterfly flower or poor man's orchid,** HH, Native American from Chile.

✳ ❚ ○ ◑

Height: 1 to 2 feet.
Colors: Pink, salmon, scarlet, lilac, purple bicolors.
Characteristics: The tumbling masses of small, delicately colored flowers bloom so prolifically they almost hide their lacy,

fernlike leaves. Each individual flower resembles a butterfly or a small orchid. Delicate patterns drawn in vivid colors appear on the top petal. The individual plants bloom three or four weeks only, so to extend the season, it is necessary to make successive sowings two weeks apart. *Schizanthus* are captivating as container plants or cut flowers, best placed where they can be viewed up close. Their cascading habit is ideal for window boxes and hanging baskets.

Cultural Information: Ideal conditions are a rich soil and cool weather. They don't mind hot days, as long as the nights stay below 65 degrees Fahrenheit. These plants are widely grown on the West Coast. It is best to pinch back the main shoot even though it then takes longer for the plant to bloom; you will be rewarded with more blooms and a less scraggly plant. They are long-lasting and unusual as cut flowers. In the frost-free Zones, 9 and 10 (see the USDA Plant Hardiness Map, page 000), directly sow the seeds in early fall for winter bloom. Space 1 foot apart.

Days to germinate: 7 to 21; *Germination temperature:* 60 to 70 degrees Fahrenheit; *Growth temperature:* 70 degrees Fahrenheit; *Days to bloom:* 60 to 65; *Weeks to start indoors:* 6 to 8.

Uses: Border, container, cool greenhouse, cutting.

Senecio cineraria; see ***Cineraria***

Shirley poppy; see ***Papaver***

Snapdragon; see *Antirrhinum*

Snow-on-the-mountain; see *Euphorbia*

Spider plant; see *Cleome*

Star flower; see *Scabiosa*

Statice; see *Limonium*

Stock; see *Matthiola*

Strawflower; see *Helichrysum*

Summer poinsettia; see *Amaranthus*

Sunflower; see *Helianthus*

Sunflower, Mexican; see *Tithonia*

Sun rose; see *Portulaca*

Swan river daisy; see *Brachycome*

Sweet alyssum; see *Lobularia*

Sweet pea; see *Lathyrus*

Sweet sultan; see *Centaurea*

Tagetes (ta-GAY-teez) **marigold, HH, very easy.** ◗ ✳ ◖ ✿ ○

Height: 10 to 36 inches.
Colors: White, yellow, orange, red.
Characteristics: Radiant, versatile, reliable, undemanding, and ever so easy to grow, marigolds are one of the most popular annuals. They were first discovered growing wild in ancient

Mexico by Cortés, who took the seeds back with him to Spain. Devout Spaniards placed their flowers at the altars of the Virgin Mary, hence the name "Mary's gold," now marigold. Marigolds became popular around the world; in India they are customarily used in leis as a symbol of friendship. Burpee has been developing better and more beautiful varieties of this easily adaptable garden jewel for over half a century.

The original marigold foliage had a pungent odor, useful in repelling insects. Some gardeners found the smell too pungent and, even though the flowers were beautiful, were reluctant to use them for cut flowers because they didn't want the odor in their house. Today there are many odorless varieties and varieties with only very faint fragrances. The roots of some Signet marigolds repel harmful nematodes and are beneficial when planted around vegetable gardens.

Through breeding and hybridization, there are many different varieties from which to choose: dwarf or tall, double or single-flowered, pungent or odorless, single or bicolored. In spite of their names, all marigolds are native Americans. The French and the African marigold names are deceiving, having nothing to do with the flowers' origins. The French marigolds are small and delicate, and the African (also called American) are tall with large flowers. There are now triploid varieties, mule marigolds (14 inches high), a cross between the big African and little French marigold, combining African vigor with a neat

Top: Torenia fournieri *'Clown Mixed'*
Above: Tithonia *'Sundance'*

French habit. The plants are unable to reproduce, so they bloom and bloom, not weakened by seed-bearing.

French marigolds are showy, trouble-free plants covered with bloom all summer until fall frost. They are ideal for flower borders, cutting, edging, and containers.

Nugget marigolds are spectacular hybrids that are the earliest to bloom, often flowering six weeks from seed. The dwarf plants (10 inches) are almost smothered with big, 2-inch fully double blooms all summer long, right up to a killing fall frost.

The white marigold 'Snowdrift' is the culmination of thirty years of research by Burpee. Larger flowered (3 to 3½ inches) than its predecessors, 'Snowdrift' is the first white marigold you'll enjoy equally as a bedding plant and for cut flowers. Plants are 22 inches high and slightly more across; the flowers are borne on long, sturdy stems and are produced from first bloom in mid-June until September.

Signet marigolds are quite different from other marigolds. The small, single flowers almost hide the foliage when bloom is at its peak: The fine, lacy foliage has a delightful lemon fragrance and is attractive even before flowering begins. The plants are dwarf, bushy, and spreading—perfect for edgings, rock gardens, and containers.

The Inca series, very resistant to high heat, is especially suited to southern summers.

Cultural Information: Marigolds take heat and drought, poor or sandy soil, and are so adaptable they almost care for themselves. They don't need—or like—an overly rich soil. They can be direct sown or started indoors. Marigolds are easy to transplant, many are quick to bloom, and resistant to disease. (However, don't overwater, because they are susceptible to rot.) They are long-lasting cut flowers. There is a wide variety available at garden nurseries; Burpee lists over fifty different varieties of seed in its mail order catalog alone. Space, according to the size of the variety, from 6 inches to 18 inches.
Days to germinate: 5 to 7; Germination temperature: 45 to 75 degrees Fahrenheit and up; Growth temperature: 75+ degrees Fahrenheit; Days to bloom: 45 to 70; Weeks to start indoors: 4 to 6.
Uses: There is a marigold for every place: edgings, border, container, cutting, rock garden.

Texas pride; see ***Phlox***

Thymophylla; see ***Dyssodia***

Tithonia rotundifolia
(tee-THO-nee-a ro-tun-di-FO-lee-a)
Mexican sunflower, HH, Native American, easy. ◗ ✸ 🌡 ❀ ○
Height: 3 to 6 feet.
Colors: Orange-scarlet.
Characteristics: Spectacular, single, fiery, dahlialike flowers 3 to 3½ inches across, on bushy, full plants with velvety gray to light green foliage. This plant is a fine accent at the back of the border, standing alone as a temporary shrub or planted as a hedge. The flowers are attractive to birds and butterflies and make good cutting flowers.

'Sundance', with its bushy habit and shorter height (3 feet), is a good performer, as is 'Torch', an AAS-winner, producing robust, bushy plants 4 to 6 feet high.

When using as a cut flower, put the tip of the hollow stems in boiling water for 30 seconds to seal, and then condition the flowers in warm water (see page 19).

Cultural Information: Any garden loam with good drainage will do nicely. The plants are heat- and drought-tolerant. Space 2 feet apart.

Days to germinate: 10 to 18; Germination temperature: 70 to 80 degrees Fahrenheit; Growth temperature: 75+ degrees Fahrenheit; (not below 50); Days to bloom: 80; Weeks to start indoors: 4 to 6.

Uses: Back of the border, cutting, hedge.

Torenia fournieri (to-REN-ee-a four-nee-E-ree) **wishbone flower,** T, easy. ✳ ◑ ●

Height: 8 inches.

Colors: Blue, pink, and white.

Characteristics: Once grown only as a summer pot plant, today this plant is equally at home in the garden or a container.

The old-fashioned variety—and the best-known—is 'Compacta' with its lavender blooms with dark, velvety blue markings and a bright yellow blotch inside the trumpet-shaped flower. However, there is also a white variety, not as readily available. Both varieties are dwarf, compact plants that are a good choice for fall color; as the weather cools, the green foliage turns a purplish color.

A new variety, 'Clown Mix', actually reminds one of a blotchy, happy clown's face with pink and purple cheeks and a wide open mouth, with a yellow strip for a tongue.

They are disease-resistant, long-blooming, and perky in a shady spot—a nice conversation piece.

Cultural Information: This rapid-growing annual prefers rich, warm, moist soil and cool weather. It will thrive along a brook or stream or will appreciate a good watering during prolonged hot, dry weather. If grown as a houseplant, the tips should be pinched back to produce a bushier plant. In areas prone to frost, garden plants can be dug and potted for continued bloom indoors. Indoors, grow at cool—60-degree Fahrenheit—nights, provide high humidity, diffused light, and very rich soil. Keep evenly moist. Space 6 to 8 inches apart.

Days to germinate: 8 to 12; Germination temperature: 70 to 80 degrees Fahrenheit; Growth temperature: 65 to 75 degrees Fahrenheit; Days to bloom: 50 to 60; Weeks to start indoors: 8 to 10.

Uses: Groundcover, edging, border.

Touch-me-not; see *Impatiens*

Trachymene (tra-kee-MAY-nee) **blue lace flower,** T, moderate. ✳ 🌡 ○

Height: 2½ feet.

Colors: Light blue.

Characteristics: Beautiful, lacy, sweet-scented flowers that have an old-fashioned romantic look. They bloom mid- to late-summer and make good, long-lasting cutting flowers. Though small-flowered, this was a favorite of Victorian flower arrangers and is considered one of the finest of cut flowers for its delicate and long-lasting beauty.

Cultural Information: This plant likes a light, rich, well-drained soil. Slow-growing, it does not like hot weather, requiring night

Trachymene coeruleus

temperatures below 70 degrees Fahrenheit to bloom, and in areas with hot summers it will not bloom until late summer. Move or transplant very carefully, as its roots are sensitive to being disturbed. The plants like crowding, which will prompt them to bloom more profusely. Space 10 inches apart.

Days to germinate: 15 to 21; Germination temperature: 70 to 75 degrees Fahrenheit; Growth temperature: 70 degrees Fahrenheit; Days to bloom: 95; Weeks to start indoors: 6 to 8.

Uses: Cutting, border.

Transvaal daisy: see *Gerbera*

Treasure flower; see *Gazania*

Top: Tropaeolum majus *'Double Dwarf Jewel'*
Center: Venidium fastuosum
Bottom: Verbena x hybrida *'Springtime'*

Tropaeolum (tro-PEE-o-lum) **nasturtium,** HH, Native American from Mexico to Peru, easy. ▲ ✹ ❁ ○ ◑

Height: Mound-shaped plants grow 1 to 1½ feet; trailing types grow to 1 to 3 feet; climbing types grow up to 6 feet.
Colors: Yellow, orange, red, copper.
Characteristics: Colorful, fragrant, single or double flowers bloom profusely all summer on a plant that almost thrives on neglect. Too-rich soil will dis-

courage blooming. Leaves and flowers are edible and are often used in salads. The leaves are round, like lily pads, and are good for using as a garnish under cheese or in salads.
CAUTION: Do not use chemical sprays on the plants you plan to eat.

There are bushy varieties and climbing varieties. 'Double Dwarf Jewel' is the most popular variety (1 foot tall) for its large, fragrant double flowers and dwarf, rounded, compact habit. 'Whirlybird' has interesting, spurless, upturned flowers. 'Fordhook Favorite' (named after the Burpee family home) is a vigorous climber with single flowers.
Cultural Information: Will tolerate dry soil but needs thorough watering during prolonged hot, dry periods. Do not fertilize as they will produce fabulous green foliage but few flowers. The seeds are large and easy to plant, fast to germinate, and good for a children's garden. Seeds are best sown where they are to grow. Cover the seeds completely, as they like darkness to germinate.

Aphids are common pests, so check for them. Space 8 inches apart.
Days to germinate: 14; Germination temperature: 65 to 70 degrees Fahrenheit; Growth temperature: 70 degrees Fahrenheit; Days to bloom: 50 to 55; Weeks before last frost to start indoors: 4 to 6.
Uses: Cutting, edging, groundcover, hanging basket, bank.

Tuberous begonia; see *Begonia*

Velvet flower; see *Salpiglossis*

Venidium fastuosum (vay-NI-dee-um fas-TEW-o-sum) **Cape daisy,** HH, easy. ▲ ✹ ❖ ❁ ○

Height: 18 inches.
Colors: Orange with purple centers.
Characteristics: Large, vibrant orange daisies, 4 to 6 inches wide with purple-black centers are set off by silvery foliage. The deeply cut leaves bear silvery hairs, like cobwebs, which make the foliage appear to shimmer. The flowers close at night. These plants are perfect for hot, dry difficult areas.
Cultural Information: These plants need nearly dry, well-drained soil. Make sure the soil is warm before sowing the seed. When germinating, it needs light. Sow in a greenhouse or sunny window in September for winter bloom. Space plants 9 to 12 inches apart. Do not water too freely; allow drying out between waterings. Cape daisy loves drought and dislikes a moist climate. These plants are especially suited to California's climate. Space 1 foot apart.
Days to germinate: 14; Germination temperature: 70 to 80 degrees Fahrenheit; Growth temperature: 70 to 75 degrees Fahrenheit; Days to bloom: 55 to 60; Weeks to start indoors: 6 to 8.
Uses: Cutting, edging, houseplant, greenhouse plant.

Verbena hortensis (ver-BEE-na hor-TEN-sis), HH, moderately easy. ▲ ✹ ❖ ❁ ○
Height: 8 to 12 inches.
Colors: White, pink, salmon, reds, purples, some with white eyes.
Characteristics: A stunning show of color, even in hot, dry sum-

mer weather, these fragrant small flowers are clustered in dome shapes. Dwarf spreading plants can create a floral carpet. A perennial in Zones 9 and 10 (see the USDA Plant Hardiness Map, page 00) but even there it is best to plant fresh each year as after a season of blooming, verbena begins to look shaggy. There are upright varieties and spreading, carpetlike varieties.

Cultural Information: This plant takes heat, drought, poor or sandy soil. Overwatering at time of sowing will reduce germination. It is best to thoroughly water the seedbed, then wait several hours or even overnight before sowing seeds. Pinch back early and more than once before transplanting for bushy plants. Mature plants tolerate dry conditions, so avoid wet locations. Deadhead to encourage new bloom and a more compact plant habit. If using verbenas as a groundcover, use hairpins to pin sprawling branches down at joints. Where a joint touches the soil, it will root, and you'll quickly increase your plants, blanketing the area with flowers.

Check periodically for spider mites. Space 10 to 18 inches depending on size.

Days to germinate: 20 to 28; Germination temperature: 65 to 75 degrees Fahrenheit; Growth temperature: 55 to 70 degrees Fahrenheit; Days to bloom: 50 to 75; Weeks to start indoors: 8 to 10.

Uses: Edging, border, ground cover, cutting, rock garden, container.

Vinca; see *Catharanthus*

Viola × wittrockiana

(VEE-o-la) **pansy,** H, easy.

🌡 ❀ ○ ◐

Height: 6 to 8 inches.

Colors: All colors, single or bicolors, blotched or faced designs.

Characteristics: Treasured for bright color and as sweet-faced companions of spring-flowering bulbs, pansies are at home in beds, borders, and containers. New hybrid varieties are bred for extra vigor and heat tolerance. Pansies are no longer only a spring-blooming flower; some varieties will bloom well into—and on occasion all through—summer.

Viola tricolor (Johnny jump-up) is a smaller plant with little flowers in solid, bicolors, or picotees (edged with a different color) that bloom from early spring to frost, so bright they seem to jump up at you. 'Imperial Blue' is an AAS-winner with the bluest large flowers, and 'Super Majestic Giant' has flowers 4¼ inches across. Burpee's 'Color Symphony' is an early-blooming mix of clear, bright colors and funny flower faces surrounded by heart-shaped foliage.

Cultural Information: Pansies will grow in any good garden soil but do best when supplemented with organic matter. Remove faded flowers and seed pods to keep plants blooming and in a more compact growing state. Continue to cut back over the summer when they become "leggy" to induce more flowers and a neater habit. Mulch may help to keep soil moist and cool. Can be sown in a cold frame in the fall in northern climates for planting out in the spring. Pansies will survive winter under a straw mulch in areas up to and

including Zone 7 (see the USDA Plant Hardiness Map, page 94). They are fine in full sun if the temperatures stay below 90 degrees Fahrenheit.

In southern climates with a long growing season, clumps can be divided. The flowers of the pansy are edible. Space plants 6 inches apart.

Days to germinate: 10 to 21; Germination temperature: 65 to 70 degrees Fahrenheit; Growth temperature: 60 to 65 degrees Fahrenheit; Days to bloom: 70 to 75; Start indoors: 12 weeks before last frost and set outdoors after heavy frost and 4 to 6 weeks before frost-free.

Uses: Edging, container, overplanting where spring bulbs will bloom.

Top: Viola × wittrockiana *'Majestic Giants Hybrid'*

Above: Viola tricolor

Wax begonia; see ***Begonia***

Wishbone flower; see
Torenia

Zinnia (ZIN-ee-a) HH, Native
American from Mexico, easy.
🌡 ❀ ○

Height: 6 inches to 2½ feet.
Colors: All colors except blue.
Characteristics: Zinnias capture
the essence of summer and make
a showy splash of radiant color.
They're versatile, too, adjusting easily to different conditions.
Flower sizes range from a dainty
2 inches to a whopping 6 inches.
Some flowers have quilled petals, some are ruffled, and still
others are single. Zinnias are
quick to grow, bloom prolifically, and withstand hot, dry
weather. They make wonderful
cut flowers, and the more you
cut, the more abundantly the
plants will bloom.

Zinnia angustifolia, 'Classic',
has masses of single, golden-
orange daisy-shaped flowers on
compact 8-inch plants that are
wonderful as an edging or groundcover. *Zinnia elegans*, Burpee's
Zenith hybrids, and Tetra Ruffled zinnias are the tallest (2½
feet and up), with flowers up to
6 or 7 inches across. Choose
'Cut and Come Again' for double
flowers on tall plants, 'Candy
Cane' for striped or flecked, bicolored flowers. 'Rose Pinwheel'
is the first rose zinnia with
mildew-resistance, a Burpee
breeding breakthrough that allows gardeners to grow this garden favorite even where summers
are humid. Blooms open pink
and turn a lovely deep rose as
the flowers mature.

Cultural Information: Zinnias
prefer well-drained garden soil
supplemented with rotted compost. A midsummer application
of 5–10–5 will help increase the
quality and quantity of blooms.
Seedlings require frequent watering but established plants will
tolerate dry spells. Better to water at ground level rather than
overhead. Pinch back plants to
encourage bushiness. Deadhead
to extend bloom.

Zinnias need warm soil to germinate, and will rot in the soil
if planted before the soil warms.
A direct sowing outdoors June
1 will be flowering by late July
and will continue well into the
fall. Space 6 to 12 inches apart,
according to the variety.

Days to germinate: 7 to 10; Germination temperature: 70 to 80
degrees Fahrenheit; Growth temperature: 60 to 70 degrees Fahrenheit; Days to bloom: 55; Weeks
to start indoors: 5 to 7.

Uses: Border, edging, groundcover, containers, houseplant,
cutting.

This page, top: Zinnia elegans *'Cut and Come Again'*
Center: Zinnia *'Rose Pinwheel'*
Bottom: Zinnia elegans *'Burpee's Zenith Hybrid Mixed'*

ANNUAL VINES

A single climbing vine may grow to 20 feet or more in height, yet use only one square foot of ground space. As such, vines are valuable even in the smallest garden, where they create an illusion of greater size. Use them on a fence or wall, to mask unsightly outbuildings, or on arbors and pagodas. Some add brilliant color to your landscape; all contribute to the "finished look" of your plantings.

Dolichos lablab (DOL-ik-os LOB-lob) **Hyacinth bean, T,** easy. ❀ ○

Height: 10 feet plus.

Colors: Purple and white flowers with dark leaves.

Characteristics: Purple or white pealike flowers appear singly or in clusters in the leaf-axles, followed by flat purple "beans." A vine that is a perennial in the tropics, it is excellent as a fast-growing screen or used on a trellis or arbor. This member of the pea family grows rapidly up to 10 feet high. It is grown as an ornamental in North America, but in the tropics it is grown for food.

Cultural Information: It likes moderately fertile soil kept reasonably moist. Does not transplant well. Will winter over in Zones 9 and 10 (see the USDA Plant Hardiness Map, page 94). It climbs by twining and needs support on which to grow. Space 1 foot apart.

Days to germinate: 14; Germination temperature: 70 to 80 degrees Fahrenheit; Growth temperature: 70 degrees Fahrenheit; Days to bloom: 90.

Uses: Background, walls, trellises, fences.

Ipomoea alba (i-po-MEE-a AL-ba) **moonflower, T,** *Ipomoea purpurea* (i-po-MEE-a pur-PEWR-ree-a) **morning glory,** H, American Native from Mexico, moderately easy. ✹ ❀ ○

Height: 10 to 15 feet.

Colors: Ipomoea alba is white, *Ipomoea purpurea* is blue, white, pink, or bicolored.

Characteristics: Moonflowers are vigorous climbing vines with full, moon-shaped, very fragrant, purest white flowers, 5 to 6 inches across, that open late in the day or early in the evening and close before noon the following day. They light up the garden at night and on cloudy days when they stay open. Their beautiful heart-shaped leaves too are large, reaching 8 inches in length. In mild climates they act like perennials. Even without the flowers, the heart-shaped leaves are attractive. *Ipomoea* is perennial in frost-free climates. The stems can be prickly, so be careful when handling the vine.

With heart-shaped leaves and trumpet flowers, morning glories can be a wonderful backdrop to a flower garden. They can camouflage unsightly buildings, trash bins or what have you. They can be trained to grow over hedges and climbing roses; grown over large bushes, they make the support plant appear to be flowering itself. They can be trained to grow down from large pots or window boxes, or even scramble along the ground where they brighten hillsides or barren land. Morning glories have tendrils that reach out and twine around netting or trellises, pulling themselves up.

Dolichos 'Lablab'

'Heavenly Blue', with 4- to 5-inch sky-blue flowers is one of the tallest, and 'Early Call', with mixed colors, is one of the shortest. 'Scarlet O'Hara' is an AAS-winner with crimson-carmine flowers, 'Pearly Gates', another AAS-winner, features enormous (4½ inch), shining white flowers.

Cultural Information: Chip the seed coat opposite the seed scar and soak overnight to speed and increase the rate of germination. *Ipomoea* is difficult to transplant, but easy to direct sow where you want them to grow. The seeds can be planted outside early, but they won't grow until the soil and air

Top: Ipomoea alba

Above: Ipomoea purpurea

Thunbergia species 'Susie'

temperatures are constantly warm. Needs some protection from strong winds. The vines climb by twining and need a support on which to grow (string trellis and fence are easy to set up). Moonflowers are sometimes listed as *Calonyction*.

Morning glories and moonflowers are popular for growing up drainpipes, mailboxes, and any other structure you would like to dress up. They can be grown together or even with other vines, intertwining to create a tapestry of colors.

Don't overwater; let topsoil dry out between watering.

The plants prefer poor, well-drained soil and will flower more if not fertilized. They self-sow easily and can become weedy. Space 8 to 12 inches apart.
Days to germinate: 7 to 21; Germination temperature: 70 to 75 degrees Fahrenheit; Growth temperature: 70 degrees Fahrenheit; Days to bloom: 90 to 100; Weeks to start indoors: 6.
Uses: Walls, trellises, fences, background.

Thunbergia alata (thun-BERG-ee-a ah-LAH-ta) **black-eyed Susan vine, clockvine,** T, Native American, moderate. ✿ ○ ◗

Height: Climbs about 5 to 6 feet.
Colors: White, yellow, orange with dark eyes.
Characteristics: This delightful little climber has arrowhead-shaped leaves. The round flowers have dark centers that contrast with light petals, hence the common name black-eyed Susan vine. These versatile vines are short enough to look good climbing up a picket fence, hanging down from a window box, or cascading over a rock wall. Can be grown as houseplants on a sunny window ledge during winter. It is a perennial vine in the tropics.

'Susie' (mixed colors) is a good choice for a hanging basket.
Cultural Information: Prefers a light, rich, moist, well-drained soil. Does not like excessive heat. Needs only moderate humidity, as high humidity causes fungus disease. Repot when roots become crowded and do not prune during growing season. As a houseplant or container plant, lightly fertilize with 7–6–19 on a monthly basis when in active growth. *Thunbergia* climbs by twining and needs support. It is attractive hanging from a container or left to sprawl as a groundcover. Space 8 inches apart.
Days to germinate: 14 to 21; Germination temperature: 70 to 75 degrees Fahrenheit; Growth temperature: 70 to 85 degrees Fahrenheit; Days to bloom: 60; Weeks to start indoors: 4 to 6.
Uses: Trellises, hanging basket, groundcover.

PESTS AND DISEASES

PREVENTION, DETECTION AND QUICK TREATMENT

The same principals for good health apply to all living things. Happily, because of their shorter lifespan, annuals are not as susceptible to disease nor as vulnerable to the pollution in large, crowded cities as perennials, shrubs or even trees. Because annuals live only for one season they do not have to fight pollution year after year. Annuals put all their energy into making flowers, which will then produce seed. They needn't store food in tubers or build strong roots to help them through the winter, as perennials do. Also, new hybrid varieties have been bred with disease-resistant traits.

Our preference at Burpee has always been for natural solutions to the problems of pests and disease. We have watched chemicals come on the market, flaunted as a "miracle control" for this or that problem, only later to learn how chemicals endanger the environment. In some cases it has happened that, after years of chemical pest treatment, stronger bugs have appeared which were no longer effectively controlled by the chemicals. Chemicals do kill pests for a time, but at the same time they kill the beneficial insects that Nature seemingly has provided for a balanced environment. So, at Burpee we try to work with Nature first and not use chemicals. In the case of annuals, we have found that chemicals are never needed. However, on occasion, even the best-cared-for gardens have problems.

Prevention: Consider our friends in nature. Harmless and friendly creatures like toads, ladybugs, praying mantises, trichogramma wasps, green lacewings, spiders and earthworms feed on the garden's enemies. They should always be welcome in your garden, for they are Nature's way of controlling pests.

The ladybug may be the greatest (although among the smallest) asset to any garden. Each ladybug each day eats many times her own weight in aphids, mealybugs, leafhoppers, fleas, lice, and other garden pests in the egg and larval stages. Ladybugs (as well as most beneficial insects) can be purchased through garden catalogs and released in your garden, where they'll stay as long as there is food for them.

At my home, it has become a tradition every spring to order ladybugs through the mail, both for the pleasure it gives our children, and for the help in our garden. Going into the garden and opening the small box filled with straw and ladybugs causes a good deal of giggling among the kids. They encourage the ladybugs to crawl on them, as they pull out the straw and place it in different parts of the garden. Our five-year-old considers them her special pets and gets excited every time she sees them over the course of the summer.

We usually order praying mantises as well. They are beautiful insects that have a voracious appetite for pests. They arrive in small (3- to 4-inch), papery egg cases, which you can hang on shrubs or from the low branches of small trees. They hatch after experiencing two weeks of warm weather. The creatures are so tiny, crawling out between the thin, papery flaps of their cases, that they leave little if any evidence of their emergence.

Ladybug

Mealybugs

Green lacewing

Praying mantis

Another little-known beneficial insect is the trichogramma wasp. Unfortunately for the trichogramma wasp, the reputation of its family name has been besmirched by stinging relatives. The trichogramma is small, hard to see, and completely harmless to humans and animals. It's not as much fun as the praying mantises or the ladybugs, so our children desert me when they arrive, four thousand eggs attached to one square inch of cardboard set at the bottom of a papercup. I have to find a warm, humid place to keep the cup until the tiny, hard-to-see, short-lived (eight to ten days) adults emerge to parasitize as many as one hundred pest eggs each. The young trichogrammas feed on the eggs of leafworms, fruitworms, cutworms, bullworms, and over two hundred other pest species.

The green lacewing is also worth knowing. It has been nicknamed the "aphid lion," a name that appealed to my children even though they didn't know what an aphid was. When the box of freshly laid green eggs mixed with rice hulls arrived, they were willing to scatter the contents around the base of plants. The green lacewings, tiny when they hatch, instinctively crawl up plants, feed for about three weeks and grow to be ½ inch long. They love what all gardeners hate: aphids, red spider mites, mealy bugs, thrips, and many different insect eggs and larvae. After they stuff themselves, they spin a white cocoon and rest for a week. Then they emerge as ¾-inch adults to lay eggs of their own and repeat their cycle.

Good housekeeping measures help your garden free of plant disease and destructive bugs.

◆ Keep the weeds down; pick up such garden refuse as dead leaves and plants. Remove old flower pots, boxes, and rotting plants from the garden area.

◆ Provide a good soil so that your plants will be healthy. Healthy plants fight insects and disease with greater success.

◆ Make sure you have good drainage throughout your garden. Stagnant water provides a breeding ground for insects.

◆ Rotate your crops. Keep notes on where you plant, and plant your flowers in a different spot each year. Rotation can be as little as a few feet from their former site.

◆ Many annuals are susceptible to tobacco mosaic. Like it or not, handling plants after smoking will encourage this virus. Likewise, smoke and ashes are harmful. As Carol Whitenack, one of Burpee's horticulturists says, "No butts about it!"

Detection: Check your plants for disease on a regular basis. Even if you work in your garden only once a week, a daily stroll through the garden, stopping to smell the fragrant flowers and perhaps picking a few for the house, will bring you close enough to spot any problems. If you catch a plant in the late stages of disease, it is best to dispose of it immediately in your trash where it can't spread infection, rather than in your compost pile.

Let the weather tell you when to look closer and check the underside of leaves and the base of plants for infestation or damage. A hot, humid, or rainy period can cause fungus and mildew that, left untreated, can spread rapidly. High winds can batter plants, damaging stems and leaves, or quickly dry out the soil. Heavy or excessive rain can flatten plants and leave stagnant water to sit around their bases, so check for drainage problems. (If poor drainage is a persistent problem, you will have to take steps to improve the soil; see page 24.) But don't get discouraged, because tomorrow the sun will shine.

Quick treatment is best: Be prepared to act quickly when you discover a problem, even a small one. Keep a first-aid kit for plants on hand. The contents will vary from year to year, as you discover what pests and diseases are prevalent in your area. It might contain an insecticidal soap, slug pellets, bags for Japanese beetles, an all-purpose biodegradable fungicide, and biodegradable insecticidal spray. At Burpee, we use and strongly recommend Safer's® and Ringer's® soaps. They are biodegradable insecticides and fungicide controls that are safe, effective alternatives to their petrochemical-based counterparts. They are designed for use both indoors and out, and are safe to use around people and pets. They also spare beneficial insects, who will continue to help you in the garden.

GARDEN DISEASES

Damping Off: Encouraged by damp, wet soil and humid air, this soil-borne fungus attacks delicate, tender seedlings. Seedlings wilt, fall over, and die.

Prevention: Use a sterile soil mix when starting plants indoors, well-drained soil when planting outdoors. Proper spacing between plants, for good air circulation, will help avoid conditions that allow fungi to grow. Before watering, always touch the soil, scratching a little below the surface, to be sure your plant needs water.

Leaf Spot: This condition occurs mostly in humid or wet weather. Spots of varied color (red, brown, yellow) appear. Sometimes, as they dry, the spots drop out, leaving holes in the foliage. Remove the infected foliage and put it in the trash to avoid infecting other plants. The disease is transmitted by rain, dew, soil, seeds, and gardeners.

Prevention: Keep the plants moist, but not wet, and avoid overhead watering. Don't work in a wet garden, especially with diseased plants; this is how the disease is most likely to be spread.

Powdery Mildew: You'll notice a dirty-white substance covering the plant when powdery mildew is present. Leaves dry out and curl, buds die before blooming. Some plants (zinnias, for example) develop mildew at the end of their growing season, when it is no longer worth worrying about.

Prevention: Give your plants enough fresh air by spacing them as prescribed on the seed packet. Good air circulation will help to avoid the damp conditions that mildew needs to flourish. Also avoid areas that are too shady when planting your flowers, if the varieties you plant are susceptible to powdery mildew. Avoid overhead watering, especially late in the day when water on the foliage does not have a chance to dry.

Rust: Cool, damp nights and humid days encourage rust, visible in raised and discolored (yellow, reddish, or orange) spots that appear on the underside of leaves, causing them to wither.

Prevention: Do not overwater and avoid overhead watering; remove infected leaves and space plants as recommended on the packet so they are not crowded and enjoy good air circulation. Check the seed packet for rust-resistant varieties of your favorite plants.

Yellows: Frequently called "aster yellows" because of its prevalence among asters, yellows is a viral disease. It attacks other annuals, too, causing yellowing around flower buds and stem tips, deforming them as they grow. The virus is dependent for part of its life cycle on leafhoppers (small, fast-moving insects) that carry and spread the disease as they feed from one plant to another. The disease could not exist without leafhoppers, and leafhoppers are unable to spread the disease if they are not reinfected every one hundred days.

Prevention: Use ladybugs and other beneficial insects to keep the leafhopper population in check. Destroy any diseased plants to prevent reinfection of the leafhoppers.

Wilt: Wilt can be caused by two different factors. It can be a physiological problem, where plants wilt from lack of water in the soil, or it can be a pathological problem, caused by fungi plugging up the water-conducting tissue in the roots and stems of the plants. The symptoms are the same: a droopy plant with downward-curling leaves. If it is a physiological problem, the water channels in the leaves and the stem quit working and go limp. The plant will recover and regain its stiffness when watered, unless it has been dry too long. To avoid this problem, water your plants regularly and deeply, and fertilize them to promote vigorous growth.

When the problem is pathological, caused by a fungus disease also called "wilt," the plants cannot recover even when watered, because the water-conducting tubes are plugged with fungus.

Prevention: When buying seeds or plants, choose varieties that are wilt-resistant. These are resistant to the fungus disease, and that eliminates the pathological problem, but no plant is resistant to being too dry. Provide proper watering.

Leaves damaged by the following pests, from left: beetles; flea beetles; caterpillars; aphids; and leafhoppers.

GARDEN PESTS

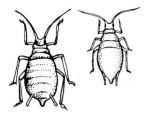

Aphids

Cutworm

Japanese beetle

Beetle

Leafhopper

Aphids (aphis): These are multicolored, pear-shaped insects. Aphids have long, slender beaks that pierce the plant tissue so the insect can suck the sap. Aphids come about ten to the inch. They multiply very quickly and can devour a plant almost overnight. However, they are fragile and suffer high mortality. You can help them to even higher mortality by spraying infected plants with a solution of Safer's Insecticidal Soap® or soapy water (two tablespoons of liquid dishwashing detergent per gallon of water.) The higher the pressure of the spray, the more you can dilute the soapy solution and have it still be effective. In the case of a houseplant, you need only wipe the leaves with a soapy solution. Wash the soap away completely after treatment to avoid damaging the leaves. If you spot ants around the plants, this is usually a sign that aphids are present. Ants feed on the honeydew that aphids secrete.

Prevention: Keep their natural enemies around: ladybugs, praying mantises, and green lacewings.

Cutworms: Black or brown and 1 to 2 inches long, cut-worms are fat caterpillars. Cutworms curl up under the soil during the day and feed on the stems of young plants at night, mostly at ground level. They can, however, also feed on the leaves and buds of mature plants.

Prevention: Plants can be protected against cutworms by means of collars pushed into the ground with sides that surround the plant stems. You can use a plastic cup, or a well-washed tin can with the bottom knocked out, or you can roll a strip of cardboard into a cylinder, staple it, and place this around the plant stem. Trichogramma wasps will also help by effectively destroying cutworms before they hatch.

Japanese and Other Beetles: Today, Japanese beetles are the bane of gardeners east of the Mississippi, and they are spreading west. They'll eat almost anything: leaves, flowers, grass, and fruit. No part of the plant is sacred to beetles. They chew the stems, leaves, and flowers, leaving good-sized holes in the leaves. After 30 to 40 days of life as adult beetles, they lay their eggs in the soil. There the larvae hatch and eat the roots of plants and grass for

approximately four months before hibernating for the winter. The next summer they emerge as beetles to continue the attack.

You can buy beetle traps at garden supply stores. These lure beetles with a natural sex attractant. The beetles fly into the trap and can't get out. Another good trap is a can of water with a thin film of oil. You can flick the slow-moving beetles off leaves into the jar, and they won't be able to fly out.

Prevention: You can eliminate the destructive pests while they are living in the lawn or garden, using Safer Grub Killer.® This powder contains bacterial spores (*Bacillus popillae*, Milky Spore Disease) toxic only to Japanese Beetles and other grubs. It will not harm beneficial insects or pets, is absolutely safe to handle, and easy to use. Best of all, it is a long-lasting measure. The spores remain active in the soil for ten years.

Leafhoppers. Wedge-shaped, small, and green, grey, or yellow in color, leafhoppers suck juices from the plant and leave it with discolored yellow leaves, stunted growth, and buds that do not blossom. They are also carriers of plant diseases, particularly Yellows.

Prevention: Ladybugs, green lacewings, and praying mantises love leafhoppers for dinner. Use an insecticidal soap early in the day when the insects are less active.

Mites: Eight-legged and borderline-microscopic, mites are easily located by their webs on the undersides of leaves. Mites suck moisture and chlorophyll from the leaves, leaving them yellow and wrinkled.

Spray or rub with a soapy solution (Safer's Insecticidal Soap® is best, but 2 tablespoons of dishwashing soap can be mixed with a gallon of water and used carefully, if washed away completely after treatment to avoid damaging the leaves). Repeat every few days until mites are gone.

Prevention: A forceful spray of water directed at the underside of leaves, done weekly, will control the mites.

Nematodes: These are most common in the South in sandy soil. They are mostly microscopic—often invisible to the naked eye—measuring $\frac{1}{50}$ to $\frac{1}{8}$ of an inch, and resembling thread- or wormlike creatures. They stunt plant growth by damaging the roots and causing the leaves of the plant to yellow, and they often cause wilt. Nematodes attack scattered plants or a section of a row. Gardeners know of the existence of nematodes only by the damage they do.

Check your roots for lobes or knots. In doubt? Send a soil sample to your state agricultural lab for testing. They will detail your nematode problem by number and seriousness, making up-to-date recommendations for control. The charge will be nominal and well worth the effort of a phone call and sample submission.

Prevention: Increase the organic content of your soil so as to attract beneficial creatures to fight your battles for you. French marigolds can be planted as a deterrent because they attract beneficial nematodes that fight the harmful ones.

Snails and slugs. Easy to spot, snails grow to $1\frac{1}{2}$ inches and slugs to 5 inches long. The difference is that snails are clothed with a shell and slugs are naked. They sport the same colors: black, brown, grey, or yellow. Both attack the foliage of plants and chew holes in the leaves. They also leave a telltale trail of silvery slime as they move.

Prevention: A ring of wood ashes, coarse sand, diatomaceous earth (coarse earth made from silica-rich diatom shells), or limestone around the plants will keep both snails and slugs away. Diatomaceous earth is used in swimming pool filters, and is readily available at swimming pool supply stores. (Snails and slugs don't like crawling over scratchy surfaces.) A bowl of beer, even stale beer, set in the ground with the rim at soil level or slightly below, will entice and drown the slugs and snails.

Whitefly. Whiteflies grow to $\frac{1}{16}$ of an inch and have very large white wings for their size. They suck plant leaves, which turn yellow and eventually fall off.

Prevention: Yellow pest strips coated with oil are available that attract whitefly; they stick to them and can't move. This is a fairly effective and pleasant way to control numbers of whiteflies, if you can manage to hang the strips discreetly out of sight. Good spacing as specified for the plant variety should be provided when planting, so that air can circulate freely. A good breeze will blow the pests away.

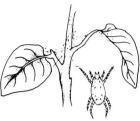

Spider mite

Red spider mite

Slug

Snail

Whiteflies

ANNUALS CHARACTERISTICS CHART

Scientific Name	Common Name	Type of Annual	Light Requirements	When to Sow	Bloom Time	Cutting	Bedding/Border	Tall/Background	Edging	Containers	Fragrance	Easy	Drying	Color
Abutilon	flowering maple	HH	PS	1	S-Fa		•	•		•				W, O, P, R, Y, Pu
Ageratum	floss flower	T	FS, PS	1	S-Fa		• (tall var.)		•	•				W, P, Br, Pu
Amaranthus	summer poinsettia	T	FS	1, 3	S		•	•				•		R, Y, G
Antirrhinum	snapdragon	HH	FS	1	S	•	•		• (dwarf var.)	•				W, Y, O, P, R, Pu
Begonia × semperflorens	wax begonia	T	FS, PS, S	1	S-Fa		•		•	•				W, P, R
Begonia × tuberhybrida	tuberous begonia	T	PS	1	S-Fa		•		•	•				W, R
Brachycome	swan river daisy	T	FS	1, 3	S		•		•	•				W, R, P, Pu
Browallia	browallia	T	PS, FS	1	S		•			•		•		B, W
Calendula	pot marigold	H	FS, PS	2, 4	Sp-Fa	•	•			•		•		Y, O
Callistephus	garden aster	HH	FS	1, 2	S-Fa	•	•		•	•		•		W, P, B, R
Catharanthus roseus	periwinkle or vinca	T	FS, PS	1	S-Fa		•		•	•				W, P, Pu
Celosia	cockscomb	T	FS, PS	1, 2	S-Fa	•	•	•		•		•	•	Y, R, P, W, O
Centaurea cyanus	cornflower or bachelor's buttons	H	FS	2, 3, 4	S	•	•	•			•	•	•	B, P, R, W
Centaurea imperialis	sweet sultan	H	FS	2, 3, 4	S	•	•	•			•	•	•	P, Pu, R, W
Cineraria maritima	dusty miller silverdust	HH	FS	2, 3, 4	S		•		•	•				Sl, P (flowers)
Clarkia amoena	farewell-to-spring	H	FS, PS	2, 4	S-Fa	•	•			•				W, P, R, Pu
Cleome	spider plant	T	FS, PS	1, 2	S-Fa			•		•				W, P, R, Pu
Coleus	foliage plant	T	PS, FS, S	1	S-Fa		•		•	•		•		R, G, Y
Consolida orientalis	larkspur	H	FS, PS	1, 4	S	•		•						W, P, R, B, Pu
Cosmos	cosmos	T	FS, PS	1, 3	S-Fa	•	•	•		•				Y, P, R, Pu, O
Dahlia	dahlia	T	FS	1	S-Fa	•	•	•		•				W, P, Pu, Y
Dianthus	pinks	H	FS	1, 4	S-Fa	•	•		•	•	•	•		W, P, R, O
Dimorphotheca aurantiaca	African daisy	T	FS	1, 2	S		•							Y, W, O
Dyssodia tenuiloba	Dahlberg daisy	T	FS	1	S				•	•				Y
Eschscholzia	California poppy	H	FS	2, 4	Sp-S		•			•				Y, R, W, O
Euphorbia marginata	snow-on-the-mountain	T	FS, PS	1, 2	S-Fa			•		•				G, W
Eustoma	prairie gentian	HH	FS, PS	1	S-Fa	•	•			•				P, B, W
Felicia amelloides	blue daisy	HH	FS	1	S-Fa		•			•				B, Pu
Gaillardia	blanket flower	H	FS	1, 2	S-Fa	•	•			•				R, Y, O
Gazania	treasure flower	HH	FS	1, 3	S-Fa		•		•					Y, O, R, P
Gerbera	Transvaal daisy	T	FS, PS	1, 3	S-Fa	•	•			•				P, Y, R, W
Gomphrena	globe amaranth	HH	FS	1	S-Fa	•	•					•	•	W, P, Pu
Gypsophila	baby's breath	H	FS	1, 3	S	•	•			•				W, R
Helianthus	sunflower	T	FS, PS	3	S-Fa	•		•				•	•	Y
Helichrysum	strawflower	HH	FS	1, 2	S-Fa		•			•		•	•	R, W, Y, P
Heliotropium	common heliotrope	T	FS, PS	1	S-Fa		•			•	•			Pu
Hypoestes	polka-dot plant	HH	PS, S	1	Sp-S		•		•	•				G, W, P
Iberis	candytuft	H	FS, PS	2, 4	S-Fa	•	•		•			•		P, R, Pu, W
Impatiens 'New Guinea'	New Guinea impatiens	T	FS	1	S-Fa		•			•				P, R, Pu
Impatiens Wallerana	busy lizzy or patient plant	T	PS, S	1	S-Fa		•		•	•				W, P, R, Pu
Lathyrus	sweet pea	H	FS	1, 2	S	•	•	•			•			B, W, P, R, Pu
Lavatera	mallow	H	FS	1, 2, 4	S-Fa	•	•	•						P, W
Limonium sinuatum	statice	HH	FS	1	S-Fa	•	•				•	•	•	W, P, Pu, Y, B
Lobelia	lobelia	HH	PS, FS	1	S-Fa				•	•				W, R, B, Y, P, Pu
Lobularia	sweet alyssum	H	FS, PS	2	S-Fa		•		•	•	•	•		W, P, R, Pu
Matthiola	stock	H	FS	1, 4	S-Fa	•	•				•			W, P, R, Pu
Mimulus	monkey flower	HH	PS	1	Sp		•			•		•		O, Y, R

ANNUALS CHARACTERISTICS CHART

Scientific Name	Common Name	Type of Annual	Light Requirements	When to Sow	Bloom Time	Cutting	Bedding/Border	Tall/Background	Edging	Containers	Fragrance	Easy	Drying	Color
Mirabilis	four o'clocks	T	FS, PS	1	S		●	●		●	●			W, Y, R
Moluccella	bells of Ireland	HH	FS, PS	3	S	●	●					●		G
Myosotis sylvatica	forget-me-not	H	PS, FS	1, 3, 4	S	●	●		●			●		B, P, W
Nicotiana	flowering tobacco	HH	FS, PS	1, 3	Sp-S	●	●			●	●	●		W, P, R
Nierembergia	cupflower	T	FS, PS	1	S-Fa				●	●				W, P, U
Nigella	love-in-a-mist	H	FS	1, 3, 4	S-Fa		●					●	●	W, P, B
Papaver	Shirley poppy	H	FS	3, 4	S	●	●					●		Y, P, S, W, R
Pelargonium	geranium	T	FS, PS	1	S-Fa		●			●		●		W, R, P, Pu, O
Perilla	beefsteak plant	HH	FS, PS	1	S-Fa	●	●					●		Pu
Petunia	petunia	HH	FS	1	S-Fa	●	●		●	●		●		W, Y, P, R, O, Pu, B
Phlox drummondi	annual phlox	HH	FS	1, 3, 4	S-Fa	●	●		●			●		P, R, Pu, W
Portulaca	moss rose or sun rose	T	FS	1, 3	S-Fa		●		●	●		●		R, O, Y, W, Pu
Salpiglossis	velvet flower	T	FS, PS	1, 3	S-Fa	●	●	●						Y, Pu, B, R
Salvia	sage	T–HH	FS	1, 3	S-Fa	●	●			●		●	●	R, P, W, B, Pu
Scabiosa atropurpurea	pincushion flower	HH	FS	1, 3	S-Fa	●	●					●		W, P, R, Pu
Scabiosa stellata	star flower	HH	FS	1, 3	S-Fa							●	●	W
Schizanthus	butterfly flower	HH	FS, PS	1	S-Fa	●	●			●				P, R, Pu, B
Tagetes	marigold	T	FS	1, 3	S-Fa	●	●	●	●	●		●		W, Y, O, R
Tithonia	Mexican sunflower	T–HH	FS	1, 3	S	●	●	●				●		O, Y, R
Torenia	wishbone flower	T	PS, S	1	S-Fa		●		●	●		●		B, P, W
Trachymene	blue lace flower	T	FS	1	S	●	●				●			B
Tropaeolum	nasturtium	HH	FS, PS	1, 3	S-Fa		●		●	●		●		W, Y, O, R
Venidium fastuosum	cape daisy	T	FS	1	S	●	●					●		O
Verbena	verbena	HH	FS	1	S	●	●		●		●	●		W, P, R, Pu
Viola × wittrockiana	pansy	H	FS, PS	1	Sp-S				●	●				W, Y, O, R, Pu, B
Zinnia	zinnia	T	FS	1, 3	S-Fa	●	●		●	●		●		W, Y, O, R, P

ANNUAL VINES

Scientific Name	Common Name	Type of Annual	Light Requirements	When to Sow	Bloom Time	Cutting	Bedding/Border	Tall/Background	Edging	Containers	Fragrance	Easy	Drying	Color
Dolichos lablab	hyacinth bean	T	FS	3	S			●				●		W, Pu
Ipomoea alba	moonflower	T	FS	3	S			●				●		W
Ipomoea purpurea	morning glory	T	FS	1, 3	S-Fa			●				●		W, R, B
Thunbergia	black-eyed Susan vine	T	FS, PS	1	S			●		●				W, Y, O
Tropaeolum	climbing nasturtium	T	FS, PS	1	S					●				Y

COLOR FAMILY KEY

B — Blue
Br — Brown
G — Green
O — Orange
P — Pink
Pu — Purple
R — Red
Sl — Silver
W — White
Y — Yellow

KEY TO SYMBOLS

Type of Annual	T —	Tender
	HH —	Half Hardy
	H —	Hardy
Light Requirements	FS —	Full Sun
	PS —	Part Shade
	S —	Full Shade
When to Sow	1 —	Start indoors
	2 —	Sow outdoors after last heavy frost
	3 —	Sow outdoors after all danger of frost
	4 —	Fall sowing in zones 9-10
Bloom/Display Season	Sp—Spring, S—Summer, Fa—Fall, W—Winter	

GARDENERS' MOST-ASKED QUESTIONS

Burpee has answered letters from customers since 1876, when the company was first formed. Some writers send praise, some send photographs of their gardens or of their children displaying their harvest, a few complain. Most letters are gardeners' questions or requests for advice. The number of letters and phone calls over the years has resulted in a large customer service department at Burpee, staffed for the most part by horticulturists who answer our "gardening hot line," helping with gardening tips, advice, and sometimes even condolences over the loss of an especially dear plant. Gardeners' thirst for knowledge is increasing; they want to know more and more. (At last count we were answering over 35,000 letters and phone calls a year.) The questions that follow are those that are the most-asked, and we hope you'll find some of the answers you seek here.

SEEDS

Q: When can I start flower seeds for my area?
A: Naturally, the timing will depend on the plant you wish to grow. Is it hardy or tender? The actual sowing date will relate to the occurence of the last spring frost and the first fall frost in your area. Study The USDA Plant Hardiness Map on page 94 to determine your zone. The last frost dates can change from one year to the next. If you observe local weather conditions you should be able to estimate the proper planting date. Most indoor planting may be made 6 to 8 weeks before the last killing frost. If you are still uncertain about sowing dates for your area, your local County Extension Services can give recommendations.

Q: What seeds could my children grow on a sunny windowsill?
A: French marigolds, 'Pot 'n Patio' asters, nasturtium, and alyssum will all grow and flower on a windowsill. Sunflowers are wonderful for children to start indoors because they are fast growers, but they will need to be transplanted into the garden when they reach 6 to 8 inches high.

Q. I had such poor germination with my seeds this year. What did I do wrong?
A. Many factors contribute to poor germination. The most common are:

1. Sowing too early in the season. Some seeds require warm, dry soils.
2. Planting too deeply. Petunia, impatiens, snapdragons and begonias, to name a few, require light to sprout.
3. Damping off. A fungus present in most soils that can kill seeds or seedlings at soil line or below. Give proper ventilation, light, and heat where necessary.
4. Forgetting to water and allowing the seed bed to dry out for even an hour can mean disaster.
5. Outdoor sowing may be washed away by spring rains or eaten by birds.

Q: Why is it difficult to germinate impatiens seed?
A: Impatiens require a little light and a warm temperature (bottom heat) of 70

degrees Fahrenheit to germinate properly. Seed should be either gently pressed into the growing medium or covered with only a thin layer of vermiculite. Enough light should filter through this thin layer to satisfy the light requirement. However, some gardeners prefer to use fluorescent lights to encourage germination. The most important steps to good germination for impatiens are bottom heat and shallow planting.

Q: When my seeds were delivered, they sat outside in subfreezing temperatures for a couple of days. Are they ruined?
A: No, a short period of freezing will not hurt your seed, unless it also gets wet.

Q: My seeds were delivered in the rain and are all wet. Are they ruined?
A: Yes, sitting in water will cause the seeds to rot.

Q. How should I save the seed of my favorite flowers, for planting next year?
A. If you save seed from hybrids, the result will be undesirable because they revert to the parent lines.

For open-pollinated flowers, wait until the flower head is completely mature (petals dried up) before you cut it from the plant. Place seed head on a paper plate to dry further, until the flower head is easily pulled apart or seeds fall free from the head. Flowers such as zinnias and marigolds have petals that will have to be removed from the seeds. If fully mature, these should rub off easily. Flower heads that have a tendency to shatter unexpectedly should have a cheesecloth netting put around them to catch seeds that may drop out. Some flowers, such as hollyhocks and sweet peas, have to have the entire plant cut and placed on a canvas to dry. Seeds are thrashed out later, so hand-pick your seed heads if at all possible.

The size, density, and shape of the seed in comparison with the plant debris will determine how you clean the seed. Sometimes screens with different size sieves are used to separate unwanted particles from the seed. Some seed can be cleaned simply by blowing the chaff away.

After the seed has been cleaned from the flower head, keep it in an airtight container in a cool spot for planting next year.

Q: I have seeds left from last year. Will they still grow?
A: Most seeds left over from the previous year will give partial germination. Seeds need to be stored in airtight containers away from heat and moisture to retain vigor. Seeds packed in metal foil stay viable longer than seeds stored in paper packets. If you want to plant last year's seeds, it is best to test a few before you waste time and effort in planting seeds that might never germinate.

You can test your seeds' germination as we at Burpee do before we package it for home gardeners. Completely wet a paper towel, wring it out and lay it flat. Distribute some of your seeds on the paper towel (these are not the seeds you will plant). Roll up the towel loosely and place it in a warm location for a few days. When you open the towel, you will be able to see which seeds have sprouted. If you test ten seeds, it's easy to figure what percentage of the seeds are viable. Eight sprouting seeds of ten means 80 percent of your seeds should germinate when planted.

Q: I grew dahlias from seed. How can I save dahlias from one season to another?
A: Dahlias store food over the summer in their roots. At summer's end, they have developed a tuber. After your first frost or when frost has blackened your plants, cut the foliage back to within 6 inches of the ground. Carefully dig up the plants, shake off soil and turn the plants upside down to drain out excess moisture. Dry out the plant tubers in the sun for 3 to 4 hours, or if necessary, a few days.

If you want to increase your stock of tubers, you may divide the clumps. However, we recommend you leave them undivided for winter storage. Pack the tubers carefully in flats or boxes and cover them with vermiculite, perlite, sand, or granular peat to prevent them from shriveling during storage. Store in a frost-free, well-ventilated place with a temperature of 40 to 50 degrees Fahrenheit. Check tubers occasionally to make sure they remain plump. A light sprinkling of water may be needed once or twice through winter. Should rotting occur, discard bad tubers and provide better ventilation and perhaps a cooler temperature.

Plant in the spring either starting indoors early or outdoors after all chance of frost. The eyes on the dahlia tubers are where the growth will sprout, therefore the roots should be planted so the eyes are facing upward. If planted with eyes upside-down, no growth will develop, or any growth will be abnormal.

Q: I have a problem with birds eating my seeds faster than I can plant them. What can I do to prevent this without harming the birds?
A: String some fishing line over the plants criss-cross fashion. It will confuse and discourage the birds. A garden blanket will also protect your seeds.

SEEDLINGS

Q: *When is the best time to thin plants?*
A: Thin plants when the leaves of nearby plants touch. With scissors or garden shears, cut the stems of the plants to be thinned at the soil line.

This keeps the roots of the healthy plants undisturbed. If the plant is easily transplantable, you can carefully dig it up and move it to another location.

Q: *It nearly breaks my heart to throw away nice little plants when I thin my flowers. Can I transplant them?*
A: Yes, you can transplant them into containers for growing on a terrace, give them

to a friend, or plant them in another area of your yard. Check "Plant Portraits" (page 37) to be sure the plants you transplant don't mind root disturbance.

PLANNING

Q: *We just moved into a new house and would like to plant some flowers to help cover the bare foundation. Our budget is limited. Are there any flowers that we can grow from seed that will return the next year?*
A: There are a few first-year-blooming perennials (flowers that return year after year) that are as quick and easy to grow as annuals. They bloom mid- to late-summer and return year after year, depending on how early you start them indoors. One of our favorites is *Coreopsis* 'Early Sunrise', because it flowers in 90 to 110 days from seed and continues blooming from early summer to frost. The Shasta daisy 'Starburst' and *Viola cornuta* ('Princess Blue') are two other good choices.

Dahlias, begonias, and geraniums can all be saved over the winter indoors and replanted the following year.

Most perennials can be grown from seed planted outdoors in July for bloom the following summer. *Burpee American Gardening Series: Perennials* will give you all the information you need for successful growing.

Q: *I have a shady spot in my yard that needs color. Will anything grow there?*
A: There are many annuals that will grow and provide color all summer in a partial-shade location. Impatiens are the most popular flower for shade, but you need not limit yourself to one plant. For added interest, try a double impatiens. Some of the lesser-known but colorful, shade-loving annuals include torenias, coleuses, nasturtiums, alyssums, mimuluses and begonias. Refer to the list on page 8.

Q: *Are there annuals that are good particularly for moist places?*
A: Bells of Ireland, calendulas, mignonette, mimuluses, four o'clocks, forget-me-nots, nemophilas, nigellas, and marigolds all like moist places.

Q: *There is an unsightly view at the back of my new yard. In time I intend to screen it out with trees and shrubs, but what can I grow fast and easily this first season?*
A: There are many good annuals that grow 4 feet or

more in a season. Some of the easiest include: cosmos, cleomes, sunflowers, and tithonia.

If you have something for vines to grow on, there are many annual vines that will disguise or cover an eyesore. Moonflowers, Mexican ivy, hyacinth beans, and morning glories grow 8 to 10 feet or more in a season.

Q: *I have a stepping-stone path that looks very bare. Is there anything that will grow between the stones?*
A: Nasturtiums, portulacas, and alyssums will grow readily in poor soil between stepping stones.

Q: *What do you recommend for a cutting garden?*
A: When planning a cutting garden, choose a few varieties that are quick to bloom: *Gypsophila*, 'Covent Garden White', and a nugget or French marigold. Then, choose a few varieties that bloom over a long period of time: nicotianas, dianthuses and phlox, and a few tall spectacular late-summer bloomers: cleomes, cosmos, asters. You can't re-

ally make a bad decision, but it would be a shame to have all of your flowers bloom together at the end of the summer, so choose some from each category: early, long-blooming, and late summer.

Q: *I used to have lots of hummingbirds in the garden, but we moved and they don't come here. Could you suggest a few flowers that might attract them?*
A: Hummingbirds love the color red, especially in trumpet-shaped flowers: petunias, larkspur, nicotianas and tithonias are a few of their favorites. Many models of hummingbird feeder are available; they hold a nectar of sugar and water that will attract the birds.

Q: *What flowers should I grow for fragrance?*
A: Fragrance runs the gamut from the honey-scented sweet alyssum, to the lemon-spicy cleome and the pungent marigold. It is a matter of taste —or should we say, smell. Try many of these fragrant flowers and see which you prefer: nicotianas, mignonette

GARDENERS' MOST-ASKED QUESTIONS

("the queen of fragrance"), nasturtiums, heliotropes, annual phlox, cleomes, sweet alyssum and stocks are a few of the many fragrant annuals. For others, refer to the list on page 22.

Q: Most annuals are not in bloom before June, and many are killed by the first frost. What can I do extend the bloom in both directions?
A: There are many cold-weather annuals that will bloom in the spring, such as larkspur, sweet pea, and forget-me-nots. Feel free to mix spring bulbs and early-blooming perennials with your annuals for early and later bloom.
Here is a list of frost-resistant flowers to extend your garden into the fall:

Abutilon
(flowering maple)

Antirrhinum
(snapdragon)

Calendula
(pot marigold)

Callistephus
(aster)

Celosia
(cockscomb)

Centaurea
(bachelor's button)

Eschscholzia
(California poppy)

Gaillardia

Limonium sinuata
(statice)

Linaria

Lobularia
(sweet alyssum)

Salvia

Viola
(pansy)

Q: We are going away for a two-week summer vacation. What can we do to protect our garden?
A: Water well before you leave, making sure water penetrates several inches into the ground. You can check this by using a trowel to dig a small hole between plants after watering to see how deeply the soil has been wetted. If your plants have developed deep root systems, they will easily be able to go for a week to ten days without additional water, unless there is high heat. Mulching will, of course, help to preserve water and retard evaporation. It is best to ask a friend to check your garden and water once if necessary. Even if you have a watering system on a timer, it is advisable to have a friend check in, in case of heavy rains.

If you take time to pick off any flowers that are past before you leave, you will help guarantee flowers when you return. This best applies to large-flower types: cornflowers, asters, and the like. Some people pick off most of their flowers in order to force the plants to work hard while they are away; the plants will greet their return with a colorful display of flowers. Perhaps picking a bouquet of flowers to take to your neighbors when you ask them to watch your garden will get you willing help (and it will stimulate your flowers to bloom on your return).

Q: How do I harvest annual everlastings such as celosias and statice for drying?
A: There are many annuals that are easy to air-dry; strawflowers, nigellas, larkspur, salvias, and cornflowers, to name a few.

Cut when the blooms are at their best and hang them upside down in small bunches (three or four stems), securing their stems with a rubber band tight enough to continue holding them as they dry and shrink. The weight of the flower heads causes the stems to dry straight. If you want curved stems or droopy flowers, you can stand them in empty glass bottles. It is important that they dry in a dark, well-ventilated room, as darkness helps preserve the flower color and good air circulation prevents mildew.

GROWING

Q: Why won't my flowers bloom? My plants appear very healthy.
A: Your garden soil probably has too much nitrogen, applied either in the form of fertilizer or fresh manures. Excessive nitrogen produces vegetative growth at the expense of flower production. Do not fertilize soils indiscriminately. There should be a reason to add fertilizers. To find out what types and quantities of fertilizer, lime, and other elements your ground needs, do a soil test (see page 24).

Q: I never have enough time to garden. To save time, could I mix soluble fertilizer into bug spray and do two jobs at once?
A: A chemist might be able to do this successfully but it wouldn't work for the average home gardener and, in fact, it could do a great deal of harm, or even kill your plants. It is very difficult to know how compatible the various ingredients in sprays and the fertilizers may be. Extremely toxic preparations might result from mixing, and we don't recommend it.

Q: What kind of weather and what kind of day are best for spraying insecticide?
A: Calm weather, with little or no wind and cool temperatures. The air is usually calmer early or late in the day. Do not spray when plants are wet or when it looks like it might rain; the water will dilute the insecticide or wash it off the plant, and your efforts will be wasted.

Avoid spraying in the middle of the day in hot, sunny weather; the foliage of the plants could be scorched or burned.

Q: I purchased several packages of earthworms through a garden catalog and now there is no trace of them. How can I get them to stay in my garden?
A: Work into your soil

compost, humus, decayed garbage, rotted newspapers. This gives worms something to eat and reason to stay in your garden area rather than foraging elsewhere.

Q: *We live in a rural area where deer can be very destructive, especially during a long, hard winter. Is there anything we can plant that they won't touch?*

A: Annuals have a better chance than other flowers of surviving an area heavily populated by deer because they grow and flower when there is plenty of other food for the deer to eat. One of our friends, Chet Davis, who gardens at Mohonk Mountain House in upstate New York, has been keeping a list of flowers that the deer in his area ignore. Here are his suggestions:

If you don't have small children, plant flowers that are poisonous (daffodils), cause rashes (*Euphorbia marginata*), have pungent smells (*Tagetes patula, T. erecta, T. signet*), rough textures (*Ageratum houstonianum, Celosia argentea plumosa, C. cristata, Gomphrena*) or are sticky to the touch (*Cleome spinosa*).

Other annuals that have survived and prospered in Chet's area are *Amaranthus tricolor. Antirrhinum majus, Begonia semperflorens, Catharanthus roseus, Cosmos* 'Sensation', *Heliotrope species, Matthiola species, Nierembergia species, Salvia species, Senecio cineraria,* and *Zinnia elegans, Z. linearis,* and *Z. pumilla.*

Chet cautions gardeners that deer could have developed different tastes in different areas, and what works for him might or might not work for everyone. He does know his deer love impatiens, pansies, asters, coleuses, geraniums, and nicotianas, without which he can't live; he continues to plant them year after year, taking his chances in the battle against the night scavengers.

Please write or call for a free Burpee catalog:

W. Atlee Burpee & Company
300 Park Avenue
Warminster, PA 18974

215–674–9633

THE USDA PLANT HARDINESS MAP OF THE UNITED STATES

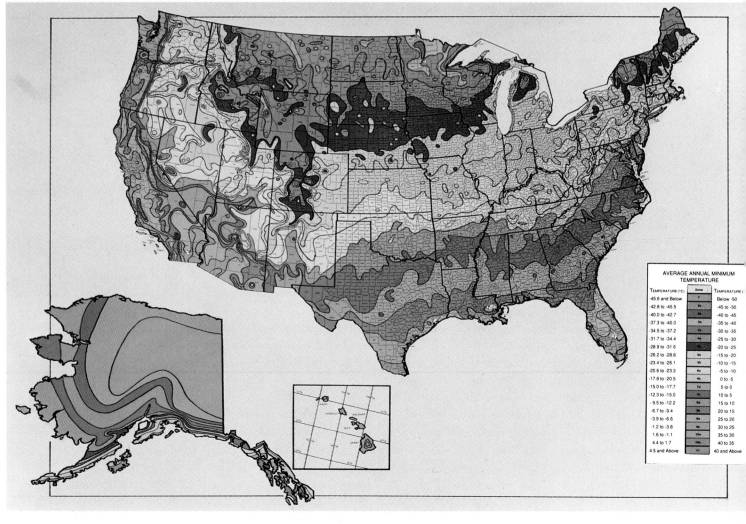

INDEX